Learning WordPress REST API

A practical tutorial to get you up and running with the revolutionary WordPress REST API

Sufyan bin Uzayr

[PACKT] PUBLISHING open source community experience distilled

BIRMINGHAM - MUMBAI

Learning WordPress REST API

First published: July 2016

Production reference: 1180716

Published by Packt Publishing Ltd.
Livery Place
35 Livery Street
Birmingham
B3 2PB, UK.
ISBN 978-1-78646-924-3

www.packtpub.com

Credits

Authors

Sufyan bin Uzayr

Mathew Rooney

Reviewer

Ahmad Awais

Commissioning Editor

Amarabha Banerjee

Acquisition Editors

Anurag Banerjee

Reshma Raman

Content Development Editor

Prashanth G

Technical Editor

Shivani K. Mistry

Copy Editor

Safis Editing

Project Coordinator

Ulhas Kambali

Proofreader

Safis Editing

Indexer

Tejal Daruwale Soni

Production Coordinator

Aparna Bhagat

Cover Work

Aparna Bhagat

About the Authors

Sufyan bin Uzayr is a writer and web developer with experience and an interest in a lot of things related to web design and development. He has worked with numerous Content Management Systems and frameworks, and writes about web design, web development, content production, branding, and typography for several blogs and magazines of repute. He also has a background in Linux administration, database management, cloud computing, and web hosting.

Sufyan is an open source enthusiast. He can code in PHP, RoR, and Perl, and is also proficient in JavaScript, jQuery, and HTML5/CSS3, as well as several other web development trends.

Sufyan primarily uses WordPress and Drupal for both personal and client projects, and often turns towards MODX for the deployment of cloud sites. He has been working with Drupal, WordPress, and other CMSs for almost a decade by now.

Sufyan is a prolific author, and has written several books on a diverse range of topics, including concrete5 for developers (published by Packt Publishing in 2014). He is associated with various publications in the field of web design and development, both in writing and editorial capacity. He has also served as the News Editor and Technical Supervisor, as well as Editor-in-Chief, for multiple web development magazines, both online and in print.

Apart from technology and coding, Sufyan also takes a keen interest in topics such as History, Current Affairs, Foreign Policy and Politics, and regularly appears on television and radio shows around the world. He is also a featured columnist for multiple journals and news publications focusing on foreign policy and international relations. Sufyan's writings on contemporary issues are simultaneously translated into different languages, and his works are cited in academic and critical journals on a regular basis.

Sufyan manages `https://codecarbon.com`, which features an assortment of useful tools and resources for web developers. Updated regularly, **Code Carbon** offers JavaScript frameworks and libraries, as well as resources related to HTML/CSS, PHP, Python, Ruby, and of course, WordPress.

You can learn more about Sufyan's writings and other non-technical works at the following website: `http://sufyanism.com`.

Mathew Rooney is a coder with multiple years of experience in the web development industry. He works with PHP, JavaScript, and offers custom-coded WordPress themes and plugins. Mathew is a firm believer in open source software and has been using WordPress for nearly 5 years.

Acknowledgments

There are several people who deserve to be this page, because this book would not have come into existence without their support.

Some names deserve a special mention, and I am genuinely indebted to:

Mathew Rooney, for the help he offered by co-authoring sections of this book. A good part of the code in different segments and chapters of this book was handled by him. Reshma Raman, for ensuring that the book stays on track, and the outline and chapter division is in the best possible shape.

Prashanth G, for editing the book, and making sure that the content is in order, and also for formatting the manuscript to make it adhere to the Packt style guide.

Shivani Mistry, for the technical edits, and for taking care of the book during the production stage.

Joe Perkins, and all the great folks at Tap Managed WordPress hosting, for offering me a free WordPress setup with no restrictions, wherein I could implement and debug the code.

Stelian Subotin, for helping me remain calm by keeping track of the theoretical aspects of the book.

Ahmad Awais, for reviewing the manuscript, and for providing his helpful insight and critical assessment.

And of course, the core contributors of WordPress, the team behind WP REST API, as well as the millions within the WordPress community -- this book would not have existed had WordPress not been there, and WordPress itself would not be so popular if it were not for the amazing community.

-- Sufyan bin Uzayr

About the Reviewer

Ahmad Awais is a senior full stack web and business development strategist with substantial industrial experience in development, design, training, and writing everything about WordPress.

He blogs at `https://AhmadAwais.com/` and tweets at `@MrAhmadAwais`. He also contributes to projects such as WP-API, WP Customize Component, WooCommerce, TwentySixteen, Easy Digital Downloads, and the WordPress, PHP, and JS Communities.

Ahmad is also one of the keenest open source evangelists; a core contributor at WordPress; a maker of lots of FOSS (Free and Open Source Software), especially WPGulp Boilerplate being used by more than 100 developers, and Sublime Text WordPress *Customizer Package*, helping about 1,000 developers write quality code with ease.

He is a published author and WordPress Content Lead at sites such as WPLift, Envato Tuts+, Torque Mag by WPEngine, SitePoint, SmashingMagazine, CreativeMarket, HongKiat, SpeckyBoy, wpMail, Post Status, WPBeginner, TheLayout by FlyWheel, ProductHunt Maker, and so on.

I'd like to thank my parents, Maedah Batool (WP Journalist) for their never-ending support; Packt Publishing, the WordPress Core Team, and the community (developers, designers, and users), without whom none of this would have been possible.

Table of Contents

Preface

The REST API is the next big thing in the world of WordPress development. Ever since its inception, it has been gaining popularity, and more and more developers are turning towards it.

Of course, the REST API comes with numerous benefits, such as the ability to interact with third-party platforms and apps. Have an application coded in Ruby and want to interact with a WordPress site based on PHP? The REST API is here to help you!

This book will help you get started with the REST API for WordPress. You will learn the basics as well as the advanced details of this new API so that you can use it in your projects.

What this book covers

`Chapter 1`, *Getting Started with REST API*, gives you an overview of what the REST API is, how it functions, and all that it is capable of doing. You will also find information about other platforms if you are new to WordPress.

`Chapter 2`, *Interacting with REST API in WordPress*, is where you will learn the basics of the REST API in WordPress. General POST and GET commands shall be covered here.

`Chapter 3`, *Working with Taxonomies and Users with REST API*, moves to taxonomies such as categories and tags. Users and user roles will also be covered.

`Chapter 4`, *Working with Forms Using REST API*, will show you how the REST API can be used to work with custom forms for your WP platform. This chapter will teach you how to get the most out of it.

`Chapter 5`, *Custom Routes in WordPress REST API*, progresses beyond default roles and teaches you how to add and work with custom routes using the REST API.

`Chapter 6`, *Creating a Simple Web App Using WordPress REST API*, is where you learn how to create a web app. Plus, you will also learn how to pass commands to your web app.

`Chapter 7`, *Mastering REST API for Your Projects*, is where you will learn how to master the REST API for your projects. Obviously, this chapter requires that you have a working knowledge of the REST API, as well as experience with WordPress development.

`Chapter 8`, *WordPress REST API in Practice*, teaches you the practical aspects of the WP REST API and its development.

`Chapter 9`, *Summing It Up*, wraps up our journey with the WordPress REST API. We will have a recap of all that we have learned so far and an overview of what the REST API can do for us.

What you need for this book

Obviously, you will need a working installation of WordPress to begin with. The latest version of WordPress is recommended so that you do not miss out on security updates.

You will also need to install and activate the WordPress REST API plugin on your site. Free download and installation instructions are here: `https://wordpress.org/plugins/rest-api/`.

At least PHP 5.4 or higher is recommended. The latest supported version of MySQL is required as well, and enhancements such as MariaDB are also allowed.

You can run WP on a generic LAMP or WAMP stack. For further instructions, consider reading the WordPress documentation.

Who this book is for

This book is for WordPress developers and designers who want to get a complete practical understanding of the WordPress REST API and leverage it to create fully featured web apps.

Conventions

In this book, you will find a number of text styles that distinguish between different kinds of information. Here are some examples of these styles and an explanation of their meaning.

Code words in text, database table names, folder names, filenames, file extensions, pathnames, dummy URLs, user input, and Twitter handles are shown as follows: "HTTP requests in JavaScript require the `XMLHttpRequest` object."

A block of code is set as follows:

```
require 'net/http'
url = 'http://www.example.com/database/1191'
resp = Net::HTTP.get_response(URI.parse(url))
resp_text = resp.body
```

When we wish to draw your attention to a particular part of a code block, the relevant lines or items are set in bold:

```
require 'net/http'
url = 'http://www.example.com/database/1191'
resp = Net::HTTP.get_response(URI.parse(url))
resp_text = resp.body
```

Any command-line input or output is written as follows:

```
$url = "http://www.example.com/database/1191";
$response = file_get_contents($url);
echo $response;
```

New terms and **important words** are shown in bold. Words that you see on the screen, for example, in menus or dialog boxes, appear in the text like this: "Hit **Preview** link in the pane and you will see your remote WordPress site in the panel."

Warnings or important notes appear in a box like this.

Tips and tricks appear like this.

Reader feedback

Feedback from our readers is always welcome. Let us know what you think about this book—what you liked or disliked. Reader feedback is important for us as it helps us develop titles that you will really get the most out of.

To send us general feedback, simply e-mail feedback@packtpub.com, and mention the book's title in the subject of your message.

If there is a topic that you have expertise in and you are interested in either writing or contributing to a book, see our author guide at www.packtpub.com/authors.

Customer support

Now that you are the proud owner of a Packt book, we have a number of things to help you to get the most from your purchase.

Downloading the example code

You can download the example code files for this book from your account at http://www.packtpub.com. If you purchased this book elsewhere, you can visit http://www.packtpub.com/support and register to have the files e-mailed directly to you.

You can download the code files by following these steps:

1. Log in or register to our website using your e-mail address and password.
2. Hover the mouse pointer on the **SUPPORT** tab at the top.
3. Click on **Code Downloads & Errata**.
4. Enter the name of the book in the **Search** box.
5. Select the book for which you're looking to download the code files.
6. Choose from the drop-down menu where you purchased this book from.
7. Click on **Code Download**.

Once the file is downloaded, please make sure that you unzip or extract the folder using the latest version of:

- WinRAR / 7-Zip for Windows
- Zipeg / iZip / UnRarX for Mac
- 7-Zip / PeaZip for Linux

The code bundle for the book is also hosted on GitHub at https://github.com/PacktPublishing/Learning-WordPress-REST-API. We also have other code bundles from our rich catalog of books and videos available at https://github.com/PacktPublishing/. Check them out!

Errata

Although we have taken every care to ensure the accuracy of our content, mistakes do happen. If you find a mistake in one of our books-maybe a mistake in the text or the code-we would be grateful if you could report this to us. By doing so, you can save other readers from frustration and help us improve subsequent versions of this book. If you find any errata, please report them by visiting `http://www.packtpub.com/submit-errata`, selecting your book, clicking on the **Errata Submission Form** link, and entering the details of your errata. Once your errata are verified, your submission will be accepted and the errata will be uploaded to our website or added to any list of existing errata under the Errata section of that title.

To view the previously submitted errata, go to `https://www.packtpub.com/books/content/support` and enter the name of the book in the search field. The required information will appear under the **Errata** section.

Piracy

Piracy of copyrighted material on the Internet is an ongoing problem across all media. At Packt, we take the protection of our copyright and licenses very seriously. If you come across any illegal copies of our works in any form on the Internet, please provide us with the location address or website name immediately so that we can pursue a remedy.

Please contact us at `copyright@packtpub.com` with a link to the suspected pirated material.

We appreciate your help in protecting our authors and our ability to bring you valuable content.

Questions

If you have a problem with any aspect of this book, you can contact us at `questions@packtpub.com`, and we will do our best to address the problem.

1

Getting Started with REST API

Ever since the middle of 2015, the WordPress community has been busy talking about the advent of REST API to the WordPress core. This is definitely a groundbreaking development and will eventually lead to bigger and better things that we as developers can accomplish using WordPress.

The WordPress REST API has been included in WordPress in a two-phase cycle, split across two versions: WordPress 4.4 and WordPress 4.5; it is not completely there in the WordPress core, but it is being added partially in a phase-wise manner.

Quite obviously, WordPress REST API (also called **JSON REST API** by some users) will play a crucial role toward the future of WordPress development, and since WordPress is the world's most popular **content management system** (**CMS**), it will contribute toward the growth of web development in general.

That said, what is all the fuss about REST API? In fact, what is REST API and why should you, as a developer, be concerned about it? Before we actually get started with coding and development, in this chapter I will introduce you to REST API, its powers, and features and what it can do for WordPress development.

Introducing REST API

Before going any further, we first need to be aware of what REST API is, why it is called so, and so on. However, let us first try to understand the concept in a nontechnical manner and then delve into the technical details.

Defining API

Since we are capitalizing the term REST API, it is obvious that it is just an acronym. The three letters **API** stand for **application programming interface**.

In simple words, an application programming interface lets you establish a connection or link between two different types of software. For instance, your computer has a USB port, which is essentially meant for connecting USB storage devices such as flash drives or USB hard disks. However, you can connect virtually any type of USB hardware to the port-printers, smartphones, tablets, and so on. As such, think of the USB port as an API for letting you connect different types of devices to your computer and allowing your computer to interact with the concerned devices accordingly. Much like a USB port facilitates the exchange of data between two physical devices, an API facilitates the exchange of data between two different types of software.

APIs have been around for quite sometime and developers and programmers use them on a daily basis. Have you ever used a third-party app to post to your social networking feed? Say, using a plugin in WordPress to tweet about your new blog post as and when you publish it? Yes, that is possible by means of API. In fact, many games and apps that rely on social logins via Facebook or Google accounts use APIs to interact with the concerned social networking services.

Therefore, the lesson here is that APIs allow developers to use content and features from a different application, service, or platform in a service, platform, or application of their own, in a secure and limited manner.

Defining REST

Much like API, **REST** is also an acronym, and it is sometimes written as **ReST**. It stands for **Representational State Transfer** and refers to a given style of API-building. Almost all the major web services, such as Google, Facebook, and Twitter, rely on REST for their APIs simply because REST is based on HTTP (which happens to be the protocol that powers nearly all of the Internet connections). Plus, REST is lightweight and flexible and can handle large volumes of activity with ease.

Therefore, REST in itself is not a new trend and has been used on the web to power services for quite a long time. Thus, for WordPress users, harnessing the power of REST API means your applications can interact with a load of services right from within WordPress, with the help of REST API.

Thus, REST is an architectural paradigm for web services, and services that use such an architectural paradigm are known as RESTful services.

The underlying idea behind REST is that instead of relying on complex web services such as SOAP or XML-RPC, a simple HTTP protocol is used for making connections. Therefore, all RESTful applications make use of HTTP requests for handling all four **CRUD** operations, namely **create**, **read**, **update**, and **delete**. This makes REST extremely versatile, and anyone can roll out their own version of REST with standard library features using the programming language of their choice, such as Perl or PHP.

Even more, REST is fully platform-independent, so you can use it in scenarios where the server might be Linux but the client can be using Windows and so on. Since it is standard-based and language-independent, a RESTful request carries with it all the information that might be needed for its execution or completion.

However, such simplicity and versatility does not mean that RESTful applications are weak in any regard. REST is powerful and can handle virtually every genre of action or request that might be expected from any of its counterparts.

Lastly, it is worth noting that much like the other web services such as SOAP or RPC, REST too does not offer encryption or session management features of its own. However, you can build such features on top of HTTP within minutes. For example, for security, you can rely on usernames/passwords and authentication tokens, whereas for encryption, REST can be used on top of HTTPS (secure HTTP). RESTful applications can function in the presence of firewalls as well.

Speaking of RESTful applications, what are some of the most common uses of REST in practice?

Well, Twitter has had a REST API since the very beginning, and for all practical purposes, it is still the most common API, being used by developers creating apps and tools that work with Twitter. You can learn more about it at `https://dev.twitter.com/rest/public`.

Similarly, Amazon's S3 Cloud storage solution too relies on REST API; for more information, refer to `http://docs.aws.amazon.com/AmazonS3/latest/API/APIRest.html`.

Flickr's API for external developers supports REST integration as well; for more information, refer to `https://www.flickr.com/services/api/request.rest.html`.

And finally, the Atom feed services, an alternative to the otherwise more popular RSS, is RESTful in its nature.

We will come back to REST later in this chapter, but first, let us familiarize ourselves with another important term, JSON.

Defining JSON

JSON is an acronym for **JavaScript Object Notation**. As the name suggests, it is a form of data exchange format that is based on JavaScript. With more and more JavaScript libraries and services coming up, JSON is rising in popularity on the web.

The best part about JSON is that it is both machine and human-friendly in terms of reading and comprehension. As a developer, you can read it and write it as much as you would work with any other programming language, whereas computers can easily parse and process it too. In fact, many popular programming languages offer their own interpreters that can parse the output to JSON and back. This makes JSON ideal for cross-platform interaction application *A* coded in one programming language and application *B* coded in another programming language can interact by converting their data structures into JSON and back, and so on.

This feature of JSON has made it a universal connector on the web. For WordPress users, JSON can also be used to replace the nearly outdated XML-RPC standard (more on this in detail in a subsequent chapter of this book).

Now that we are aware of what the terms API, REST, and JSON stand for, let us come back to REST API and start by first learning more about the REST API in itself. Thereafter, we will focus on what it can do for WordPress developers and then get started with is usage in WordPress.

So, what can REST API do or, in other words, how has it been proving to be useful?

Using REST API in real-world applications

REST API has become the talk of the town in the WordPress community only fairly recently. However, it has been around for quite a long while, and RESTful services are, in fact, as old as the Internet itself.

We are aware that the Internet is made up of different computers and servers, speaking different languages and running different services and processes. As such, a common protocol has been evolved to enable such different services and processes to communicate with each other. Such protocols can be described as a set of given standards that allow for Internet communication in a given manner.

Now, REST API, in itself, sits on top of such protocols, and enables us to facilitate communication between different services and machines and helps us interpret the data exchange that might be ongoing between two different services. There are many other such services that do the same job as REST, but with a difference of their own. For instance, JMS is a similar technique exclusive to Java applications, whereas XML-RPC is a capable, popular, but slightly dated and less secure methodology that can facilitate communication between services, much like REST.

Advantages of REST services

So, what makes REST better? In simplest of terms, REST helps in data exchange with a set of well-established mechanisms and protocols and focuses more on minimum workload, unlike many other similar methods that are heavier and bulkier in terms of operation. As such, REST focuses more on efficiency and speed and offers cross-platform data exchange. This is, by far, the biggest advantage of using RESTful services.

Now, as the Internet expands, so do the devices and technologies associated with it. With more and more mobile devices coming to the fore and coding standards being curated to adhere to specific norms, REST APIs too are evolving in order to meet purer standards of implementation. Thus, while the implementation of REST API remains more or less uniform, the modus operandi of RESTful services coded in different languages or platforms can have some minor differences. This is obvious to some extent because REST is an architectural style and not an architectural standard, and unlike HTML5, you cannot expect a W3C compliant guideline for REST API.

Now that we have covered the basic details about REST API and its major benefits, it is time to actually get started with REST in practice. In the next section, I will now talk a bit about how REST requests and responses work across different platforms and languages. Plus, the coming section will also be discussing the basic functioning of REST, including how simple and complex requests work. This, of course, is more of a practical consideration and less of a puritan one, and you can skip the coming section and move straight on to WordPress REST API if you want, but for the sake of information and for those who might be interested in learning more about REST API across different services and platforms, let us discuss REST properly before heading toward its relation with WordPress.

Key considerations when working with REST

Before we go any further ahead, let us discuss some key considerations that are useful to bear in mind when working with RESTful applications and services.

Since REST is an architectural style and not a standard, the following are considerations and not totally mandatory rules.

When working with WordPress, the following key considerations are something you should bear in mind. The question is, why so?

It is because many times you will be using REST API to communicate with services that may not be running on WordPress (for example, a third-party social network that your plugin might interact with). As such, if you follow the following norms when working with REST API in WordPress, you won't have to face issues with uniformity.

Architectural components in REST

The architecture of RESTful services is pretty straightforward and we can briefly summarize its main components as follows:

- *Resources* are the key components of RESTful services. They are identified by logical URLs and are universally accessible by other parts of the system.
- Resources should contain *links* to other information, much like web pages. Thus, resources should be interconnected.
- Resources can be cached.

Since HTTP is what RESTful services used, the HTTP cache-control headers are sufficient for this task.

- RESTful systems follow the client-server model.
- Standard HTTP proxy servers can be used in RESTful architecture.
- REST services can interact with non-REST services, and vice versa.

Design principles in REST

REST is more of a style and less of a standard, so there are not many design principles to consider. In general, this is what you should follow:

- GET requests should not cause a change in state or alter data. If you wish to modify the state or data, use POST requests.
- Pagination is always a good practice; if your GET query reads entries, let it read the first N number of entries (for example, 20) and then use links to read more entries.
- Physical URLs are considered a bad practice, and logical URLs should be preferred.
- If the REST response is in XML, consider using a schema.

Also, for documenting a REST service, you can use **Web Services Description Language** (**WSDL**) or **Web Applications Description Language** (**WADL**). Both are feature-rich, but WSDL offers more flexibility as it does not bind itself to **Simple Mail Transfer Protocol** (**SMTP**) servers, whereas WADL is easier to read and interpret. And if either of them does not appeal to you, a simple HTML document too can suffice.

Getting started with REST implementation

We are now familiar with REST API and JSON. Plus, we also know that REST API is indeed useful in many different ways. Let us now try to put it into practice.

Passing commands in SOAP versus REST

Say, we need to query a given database for user details of a user with `ID 1191`. Using web services and **Simple Object Access Protocol** (**SOAP**), we will be doing something such as the following:

```
<?xml version="1.1"?>
<soap:Envelope
xmlns:soap="http://www.w3.org/2001/12/soap-envelope"
soap:encodingStyle="http://www.w3.org/2001/12/soap-encoding">
<soap:body pb="http://www.example.com/database">
<pb:GetUserDetails>
<pb:UserID>1191</pb:UserID>
</pb:GetUserDetails>
</soap:Body>
```

```
</soap:Envelope>
```

The preceding code will give us an embedded XML file inside a SOAP response envelope.

And how will we do this using REST? The following way: `http://www.example.com/database/UserDetails/1191`.

Yes, that is all. It is a simple URL with GET request, and the response will give us the raw data, that is, the details of the user with ID `1191`. While in SOAP, we needed multiple libraries to parse the response, in REST, we just need to pass the simple URL. We can even test the API directly right within the browser as a simple request.

Of course, the preceding example is a simplified case, and if need be, REST libraries do exist. However, as it becomes clear, REST is way simpler than web services and other counterparts.

TIP

Downloading the example code
You can download the example code files for this book from your account at `http://www.packtpub.com`. If you purchased this book elsewhere, you can visit `http://www.packtpub.com/support` and register to have the files e-mailed directly to you.
You can download the code files by following these steps:

1. Log in or register to our website using your e-mail address and password.
2. Hover the mouse pointer on the **SUPPORT** tab at the top.
3. Click on **Code Downloads & Errata**.
4. Enter the name of the book in the **Search** box.
5. Select the book for which you're looking to download the code files.
6. Choose from the drop-down menu where you purchased this book from.
7. Click on **Code Download**.

You can also download the code files by clicking on the **Code Files** button on the book's webpage at the Packt Publishing website. This page can be accessed by entering the book's name in the **Search** box. Please note that you need to be logged in to your Packt account.

Once the file is downloaded, please make sure that you unzip or extract the folder using the latest version of:

- WinRAR / 7-Zip for Windows
- Zipeg / iZip / UnRarX for Mac
- 7-Zip / PeaZip for Linux

TIP

The code bundle for the book is also hosted on GitHub at `https://github.com/PacktPublishing/Learning_WordPress_REST_API`. We also have other code bundles from our rich catalog of books and videos available at `https://github.com/PacktPublishing/`. Check them out!

Handling data in REST

For complex operations, the methodology remains similar. Let us refine the preceding query and look for the user with first name `Sample` and last name `User` as follows: `http://www.example.com/database/UserDetails?firstName=Sample&lastName=User`.

As we can see, for longer parameters, we are including the parameters within the body of the HTTP POST request. At this point, it is useful to discuss REST requests in themselves.

For simpler queries of a read-only nature, GET is the de facto standard. However, for read-only queries that are complex in nature, POST requests can be used. Of course, POST requests are also used for queries that can change the state of the data and deal with creation, updating, and deletion of data.

If you are wondering how to distinguish a simple query from a complex one, consider this: when reading a blog, you send a GET request as a simple query to open the page, but if you decide to post a comment on the blog post or share it via any of the social networks, you send a POST request with additional and more complex details.

And in terms of server responses, RESTful services can handle XML, CSV, and JSON. Each of these formats has its own advantages: XML, for example, is pretty easy to expand, CSV is compact and lightweight, whereas JSON is easy to parse. As you might have guessed by now, for WordPress REST API, JSON is the way to go, all thanks to JavaScript.

Unless the response needs to be read by humans, HTML is not the de facto choice for REST server responses. Of course, since almost everything on the World Wide Web needs to be read by humans, HTML is being used as a server response for RESTful services.

Using REST in different programming languages

As the final part of our discussion on REST and RESTful services, before we dive toward WordPress and start the next chapter, let us take a look at usage and implementation of REST in different programming languages. If you are an existing WordPress developer and are well-versed with PHP, you might wish to skip this section and move ahead. However, for the benefit of those who might have migrated to WordPress development or those who are familiar with some other popular web development language, I have provided the methods for sending GET and POST requests via HTTP in the programming languages that I know of.

Let us begin with Ruby.

Ruby

In Ruby, you can send HTTP requests using the `Net::HTTP` class. Thus, for GET requests, to look up the record number `1191` from the database of `example.com`, this is how you should do it:

```
require 'net/http'
url = 'http://www.example.com/database/1191'
resp = Net::HTTP.get_response(URI.parse(url))
resp_text = resp.body
```

In the preceding example, we are using an object to handle the HTTP response code.

Similarly, for POST requests:

```
require 'net/http'
url = 'http://www.example.com/database/user'
params = {
firstName =>'Sample',
lastName =>'User'
}
resp = Net::HTTP.post_form(url, params)
resp_text = resp.body
```

Here again, we are using `Net::HTTP` class and using the `post_form` method for POSTing.

Python

In Python, we already have the `urllib2` module, so for RESTful actions, we just need to pass the GET request and then handle the response.

For example:

```
import urllib2
url = 'http://www.example.com/database/1191'
response = urllib2.urlopen(url).read()
And for POST requests, we will once again rely on the urllib2 module:
import urllib
import urllib2
url = 'http://www.example.com/database/user'
params = urllib.urlencode({
'firstName': 'Sample',
'lastName': 'User'
})
response = urllib2.urlopen(url, params).read()
```

In the preceding code, we are passing the request data as an extra parameter.

Perl

Personally, I have always relied on `LWP`, the library for **WWW** in Perl, for REST requests via HTTP.

For example, a GET request would look something like the following:

```
use LWP::Simple;
my $url = 'http://www.example.com/database/1191';
# sample request
my $response = get $url;
die 'Error getting $url' unless defined $response;
```

The preceding code is sufficient for a GET request without additional headers. For something more complex, you should consider creating a browser object in Perl and then handling it accordingly as follows:

```
use LWP;
my $browser = LWP::UserAgent->new;
my $url = 'http://www.example.com/database/1191';
my $response = $browser->get $url;
die 'Error getting $url' unless $response->is_success;
print 'Content type is ', $response->content_type;
print 'Content is:';
```

```
print $response->content;
```

Now, if you need to issue a POST request, you can follow the preceding approach again, and create a browser object and then pass the POST request as follows:

```
my $browser = LWP::UserAgent->new;
my $url = 'http://www.example.com/database/1191';
my $response = $browser->post($url,
[
'firstName' =>'Sample',
'lastName' =>'User'
];
);
die 'Error getting $url' unless $response->is_success;
print 'Content type is ', $response->content_type;
print 'Content is:';
print $response->content;
```

In the preceding example, we are using the browser object for issuing the POST request and then mapping the field names directly to the values.

For working with complex REST operations in Perl, you should consider learning more about `LWP` (the library for `www` in Perl).

C#

C# as a programming language has structures and concepts of its own. For all practical purposes, you will need to use the .NET classes `HttpWebRequest` and `HttpWebResponse` for handling REST requests sent via HTTP.

For example, the following is what a typical GET request in C# would look like:

```
static string HttpGet(string url) {
HttpWebRequest req = WebRequest.Create(url)
as HttpWebRequest;
string result = null;
using (HttpWebResponse resp = req.GetResponse()
as HttpWebResponse)
{
StreamReader reader =
new StreamReader(resp.GetResponseStream());
result = reader.ReadToEnd();
}
return result;
}
```

What does the preceding code do? It simply passes a request and then returns the entire response as one long string. For backward compatibility, I would suggest that if you are passing parameters with your requests, it is advisable to properly encode them. You can use any of the native C# classes or methods for such encoding.

For passing POST requests, the method is similar to GETing, as shown in the following:

```
static string HttpPost(string url,
string[] prName, string[] prVal)
{
HttpWebRequest req = WebRequest.Create(new Uri(url))
as HttpWebRequest;
req.Method = "POST";
req.ContentType = "application/x-www-form-urlencoded";

// Creating a string, encoded and with all parameters
// Assuming that the arrays prName and prVal are of equal length
StringBuilder przz = new StringBuilder();
for (int i = 0; i < prName.Length; i++) {
przz.Append(prName[i]);
przz.Append("=");
przz.Append(HttpUtility.UrlEncode(prVal[i]));
przz.Append("&");
}

// Encoding the parameters
byte[] frDat =
UTF8Encoding.UTF8.GetBytes(przz.ToString());
req.ContentLength = frDat.Length;

// Sending the request
using (Stream post = req.GetRequestStream())
{
post.Write(frDat, 0, frDat.Length);
}

// Getting the response
string result = null;
using (HttpWebResponse resp = req.GetResponse()
as HttpWebResponse)
{
StreamReader reader =
new StreamReader(resp.GetResponseStream());
result = reader.ReadToEnd();
}

return result;
}
```

Once again, we have encoded the parameters in the preceding code and have accepted a request and returned the response.

Java

When using REST requests in Java, the concept is similar to that of C#, and an experience Java coder can easily pick up the ropes. Basically, you use the `HttpURLConnection` class and invoke its object type. Following is an example for a GET request:

```
public static String httpGet(String urlStr) throws IOException {
URL url = new URL(urlStr);
HttpURLConnection conn =
(HttpURLConnection) url.openConnection();
if (conn.getResponseCode() != 200) {
throw new IOException(conn.getResponseMessage());
}
// Buffering the result into a string
BufferedReader drdr = new BufferedReader(
new InputStreamReader(conn.getInputStream()));
StringBuilder sb = new StringBuilder();
String line;
while ((line = drdr.readLine()) != null) {
sb.append(line);
}
drdr.close();
conn.disconnect();
return sb.toString();
}
```

In the preceding code, we are issuing a GET request and then accepting the response as one long string. If you wish to use it in your projects, you might wish to tweak it a bit, probably with the help of `try` or `catch`. Plus, note that for backward compatibility, it is advisable to encode the parameters that are passed with the request URL.

Now, for POST requests, this is how we will work:

```
public static String httpPost(String urlStr, String[] prName,
String[] prVal) throws Exception {
URL url = new URL(urlStr);
HttpURLConnection conn =
(HttpURLConnection) url.openConnection();
conn.setRequestMethod("POST");
conn.setDoOutput(true);
conn.setDoInput(true);
conn.setUseCaches(false);
```

```
conn.setAllowUserInteraction(false);
conn.setRequestProperty("Content-Type",
"application/x-www-form-urlencoded");

// Creating form content
OutputStream out = conn.getOutputStream();
Writer writer = new OutputStreamWriter(out, "UTF-8");
for (int i = 0; i < prName.length; i++) {
writer.write(prName[i]);
writer.write("=");
writer.write(URLEncoder.encode(prVal[i], "UTF-8"));
writer.write("&");
}
writer.close();
out.close();

if (conn.getResponseCode() != 200) {
throw new IOException(conn.getResponseMessage());
}

// Buffering the result into a string
BufferedReader drdr = new BufferedReader(
new InputStreamReader(conn.getInputStream()));
StringBuilder bsbs = new StringBuilder();
String line;
while ((line = drdr.readLine()) != null) {
bsbs.append(line);
}
drdr.close();

conn.disconnect();
return bsbs.toString();
}
```

Once again, we are accepting a POST request with a parameter and then passing the response accordingly.

> You will need to supplement this code with `try/catch` structures before inserting it within your projects.

Also, an experienced Java coder will be aware that Java is not the most popular language for web development and that its support for handlers for web connections is not at the top of its league. It is, therefore, a good idea to make use of packages and handlers from the Apache library for this purpose. However, we will evade this discussion now since it is beyond the scope of this book, and Java code is of little merit for someone whose primary focus might be on using RESTful services with WordPress.

PHP

Now, finally, we come to the language in which WordPress has been coded. Using REST in PHP is very easy because even the most basic PHP functions with a file-access model can work seamlessly with HTTP requests and URLs.

Therefore, for GET requests, virtually any file-reading function of PHP can do the job, such as `fopen`, for example:

```
$url = "http://www.example.com/database/1191";
$response = file_get_contents($url);
echo $response;
```

If you are passing parameters with GET requests, it might be a good idea to encode them.

However, while GET requests are pretty easy to handle, POST requests require a bit of work because you need to open a connection to the target server and then send the HTTP header information. For example, consider the following code:

```
function httpRequest($host, $port, $method, $path, $prms){
// prms is to map from name to value
$prmstr = "";
foreach ($prms as $name, $val){
$prmstr .= $name . "=";
$prmstr .= urlencode($val);
$prmstr .= "&";
}
// Assign defaults to $method and $port
if (empty($method)) {
$method = 'GET';
}
$method = strtoupper($method);
if (empty($port)) {
$port = 80; // Default HTTP port
}

// Create the connection
$sock = fsockopen($host, $port);
```

```
if ($method == "GET") {
$path .= "?" . $prmstr;
}
fputs($sock, "$method $path HTTP/1.1\r\n");
fputs($sock, "Host: $host\r\n");
fputs($sock, "Content-type: " .
"application/x-www-form-urlencoded\r\n");
if ($method == "POST") {
fputs($sock, "Content-length: " .
strlen($prmstr) . "\r\n");
}
fputs($sock, "Connection: close\r\n\r\n");
if ($method == "POST") {
fputs($sock, $prmstr);
}
// Buffer the result
$result = "";
while (!feof($sock)) {
$result .= fgets($sock,1024);
}
fclose($sock);
return $result;
}
```

Now, using the preceding sample function, we can issue a POST request as follows:

```
$resp = httpRequest("www.example.com",
80, "POST", "/Database",
array("firstName" =>"Sample", "lastName" =>"User"));
```

We can also use the **client URL request library** (**cURL**) when working with RESTful requests in PHP.

JavaScript

Having covered all of that, let us finally discuss REST implementation in JavaScript. We will be saving the JSON issue for detailed discussion during the course of this book, so let's just focus on the traditional route now.

REST requests can be sent from client-side or in-browser JavaScript. If you have ever worked with an AJAX application, you have followed the REST design principles to a great extent, with the response being in JSON.

HTTP requests in JavaScript require the `XMLHttpRequest` object. The following function is a simple way to create the object:

```
function createRequest() {
var result = null;
if (window.XMLHttpRequest) {
result = new XMLHttpRequest();
if (typeof xmlhttp.overrideMimeType != 'undefined') {
result.overrideMimeType('text/xml'); // Or anything else
}
}
else if (window.ActiveXObject) {
result = new ActiveXObject("Microsoft.XMLHTTP");
}
return result;
}
```

Now that you have created the object, you are ready to send HTTP requests. However, the `XMLHttpRequest` object, while it can send requests, cannot return values by default. So it is better to have a callback function that can be invoked when your request is completed.

Thereafter, you are ready to send the request. For a GET request, the approach is fairly simple:

```
req.open("GET", url, true);
req.send();
And for POST requests:
req.open("POST", url, true);
req.setRequestHeader("Content-Type", "application/x-www-form-urlencoded");
req.send(form-encoded request body);
```

As you can see, sending HTTP requests in JavaScript is pretty easy and you just need to call the appropriate function.

REST API in WordPress

So, now that we have seen the benefits and features of REST API and also learned a bit about JSON, how exactly can it be useful for WordPress developers?

Well, there is a lot that REST API can do in WordPress.

To begin with, the WordPress REST API is revolutionary in the sense it can help us build new applications with WordPress. Specialized editors, site management tools, and more can be created and run even without a custom API and without a companion plugin being installed on the WordPress website. As such, a WordPress theme can use the REST API to load content dynamically, and practically speaking, WordPress in itself can function as a full-fledged architectural framework.

Let us see some of the major benefits that REST API brings to the world of WordPress.

Universality

WordPress has had an API of its own for quite a while, and as such, the *API* part is nothing new for WordPress developers. In fact, if you have ever coded a plugin for WordPress, you might already be aware that WordPress uses its API to interact with the plugin.

However, the old WordPress API is ideal for internal processes such as a plugin, but hardly useful for external services. REST API, on the other hand, is perfect for allowing WordPress to interact with services outside of WordPress.

In other words, with REST API on board, WordPress can interact with services and websites on the Internet, which may or may not use WordPress! Yes, WordPress REST API can interact and exchange information with any service on the web that might be coded in a different language, running a different code structure, or be of a different nature.

Similarly, you can also let external services interact with WordPress content with the help of REST API. Thus, any service or website making use of REST API can now interact with your WordPress website and its posts, pages, custom post types, taxonomies, users, and more with ease, as long as it runs on the HTTP protocol (which is supported by nearly all of the Internet nowadays).

In HTTP, the POST, GET, UPDATE, and DELETE requests will allow you to create, read, update, and delete content, respectively. We shall revisit these steps with code examples in later chapters of this book, as we progress through our journey with REST API in WordPress.

Remote management

WordPress REST API comes with safety measures of its own, such as cookie-based and OAuth authentication.

Cookie-based authentication is useful for plugins and themes, whereas OAuth authentication (relying on `http://oauth.net/`) can be used to authenticate desktop, mobile, and web clients. This will allow WordPress REST API to define limited and clearly defined data exchange; the external service will be able to view and edit only that section of data that is made available to it, nothing else.

> Notice the terms *desktop*, *mobile*, and *web clients* in the preceding paragraph; REST API enables remote management for WordPress. You can manage your WordPress website from a desktop client installed on your computer or a mobile application, without actually having to visit the WordPress admin panel at all!

As such, you can build clients that let you create and publish a blog using WordPress, but offer a minimal and more interactive interface than the WordPress admin panel. Since JSON is natively supported by both Android and iOS, WordPress REST API is a special boon for mobile developers who can build mobile applications that make use of REST API for interacting with WordPress platforms while running on Android or iOS.

Third-party support

As already stated, REST API enables WordPress to interact with services and sites that might not be built on WordPress, and vice versa. However, what can we expect from such cross-platform and third-party support?

Well, this means we can now procure content and interact with data from any other platform as long as we follow the HTTP route. For example, we can now allow **Ruby on Rails** (**RoR**) applications to interact with WordPress websites, while WordPress too can interact with systems that are otherwise not coded in PHP.

This is especially useful for folks who are working with third-party tools and need to interact with WordPress regularly. Furthermore, frontend developers can now focus on the frontend of their website without having to worry about the backend, all thanks to WordPress REST API.

Even more so, REST API can be used by WordPress developers to take their plugin and themes to non-WordPress platforms and other CMSs.

Summary

It is obvious that REST API is a path breaking and revolutionary innovation that has the ability to transform how we code with WordPress. With better interaction and collaboration across multiple platforms and services, REST API can help us build better and more useful applications in WordPress and do more with our development workflow.

Over the course of the next chapters of this book, you will learn how to use REST API to interact with WordPress and create, read, edit, and delete data. Plus, you will also learn how to deal with taxonomies and users, as well as custom routes and create web apps using WordPress REST API. We will discuss the basics of working with and extending the default routes used by WordPress REST API, as well as creating our own endpoints.

I hope this book will prove useful in helping you learn more about and master WordPress REST API as well as tapping its potential to the fullest in order to benefit from the many new features that REST API brings to the table.

Summary

2

Interacting with REST API in WordPress

In the previous chapter, we became familiar with the basics of REST API, how RESTful services work, and how to issue and manage basic REST commands in different languages and using different methods.

Now that the introduction is out of the way, it is time for us to actually get started with REST API in WordPress. In the last chapter, we have seen the benefits of using REST API in WordPress and all that it can bring to the table in terms of features.

Starting from this chapter, we will now be seeing how to use REST API when working with WordPress. This chapter will introduce you to basic GET and POST requests and then will teach you how to deal with posts in WordPress via REST API. Furthermore, you will also learn how to handle posts, post metadata or meta fields, and then copy posts from one remote site to another.

Getting started

First up, you will need to set up your WordPress website. Obviously, you should not use a production site for learning purposes; therefore, I will strongly advise you to set up a test installation of WordPress for experimenting and playing with REST API. Depending on your mode of operation, you may choose to do it the way it suits you—some developers prefer having a local version of WordPress running on their device, whereas others, such as myself, set up WordPress live on a test server and access it accordingly.

You might also do it via Vagrant, if that suits you.

You may then install the WordPress REST API plugin much like any other normal plugin. Find the latest version at `https://wordpress.org/plugins/rest-api/`.

That said, let us get started with REST requests in WordPress. As we have seen in the last chapter, REST requests generally revolve around the four common HTTP transport methods: GET, PUT, POST, and DELETE. Plus, we have also learned that GET and POST requests are used to obtain data and to update data, respectively.

Furthermore, we are, by now, aware that RESTful requests are pretty simple in nature, and it is only a matter of passing the right URL string as the parameter in order to make GET or POST queries. You can directly pass the URL strings, or place them within functions, or use a service or tool such as Postman to do it. In this chapter, we will be discussing all three methods.

Issuing requests via Postman

The biggest and most obvious advantage of Postman is that it allows you to turn requests into code snippets that you can use and reuse within your code. Thus, Postman can be used to export requests as JavaScript, and that makes it the perfect fit when working with REST API for WordPress or web development.

Postman lets you send authenticated requests in a native manner. In Google Chrome, once you have installed and activated the Postman extension, you can start sending HTTP requests.

Postman supports multiple HTTP requests, and you can see that directly in the drop-down menu.

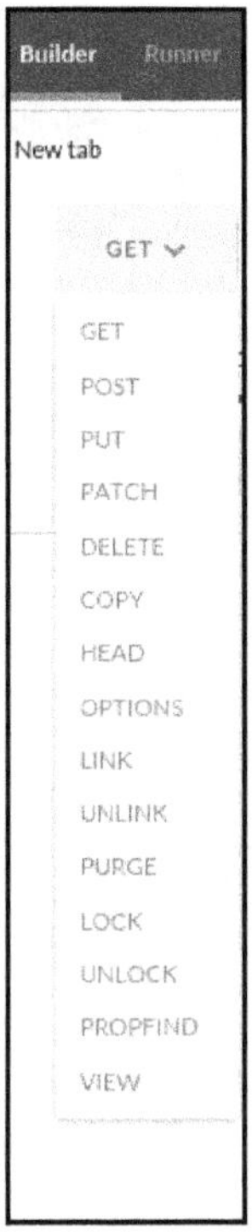

Of course, for our purpose, the **GET** and **POST** requests are the most important.

To issue an HTTP request via Postman, you need to enter the URL value and specify the parameters, if any. For instance, a **GET** request to a sample URL would look like as shown in the following screenshot:

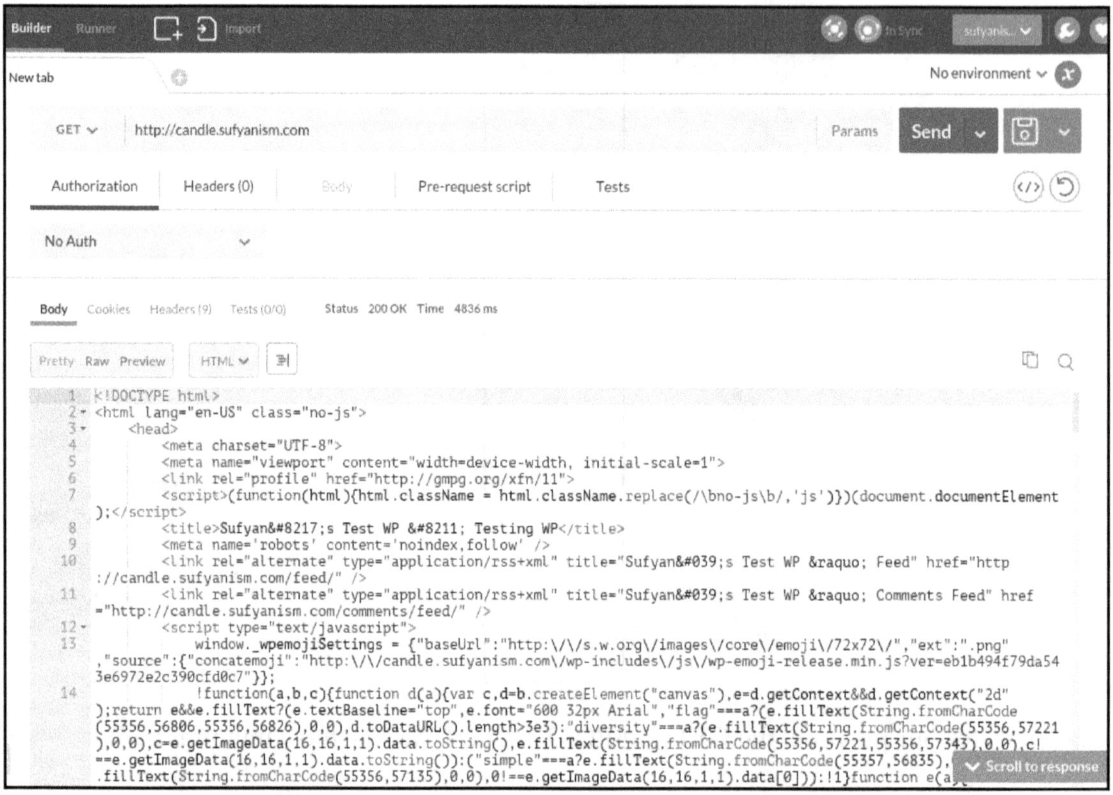

The preceding requests give us raw response in HTML code. You can also see the same response in JSON, XML, or text format. However, did our GET request actually fetch our WordPress site? Simply hit the **Preview** link in the pane and you will see your remote WordPress site in the panel.

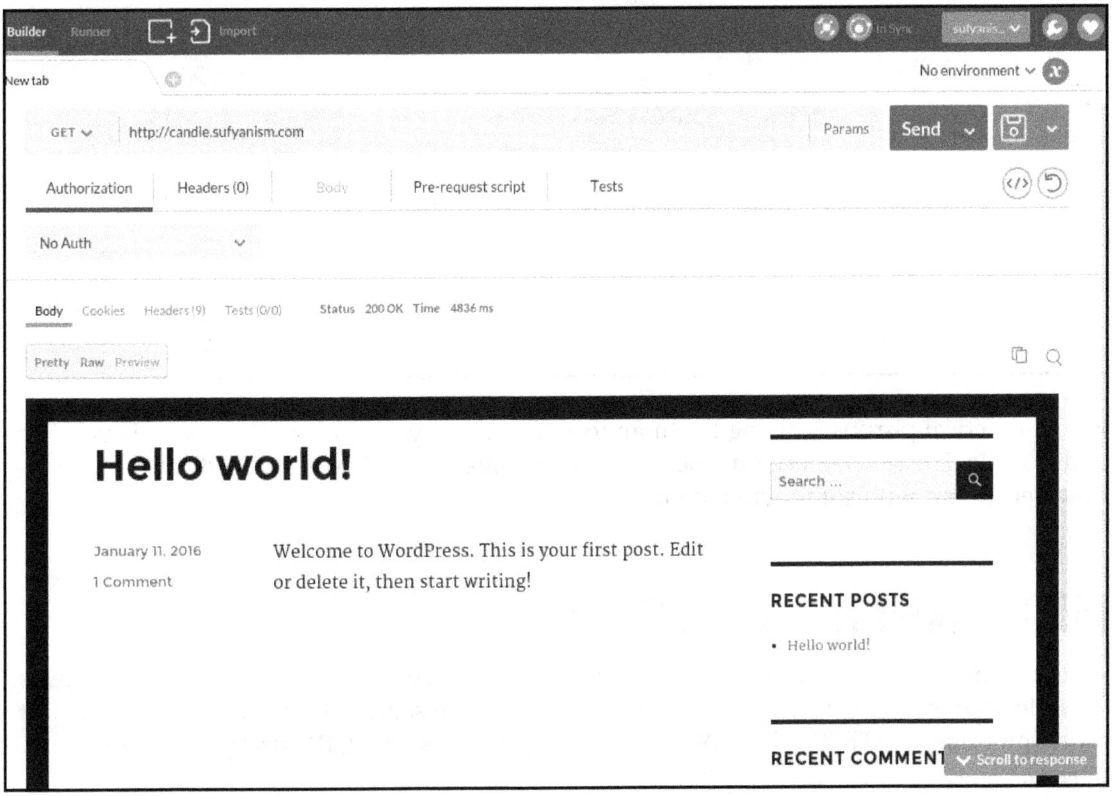

This is a pretty basic HTTP request and you are just fetching the WordPress site as it is. Since we will be using REST API for bigger and better queries, why not try such a request using Postman?

Say, we wish to login to our remote WordPress site. You can access the `wp-admin` of your site in a similar manner.

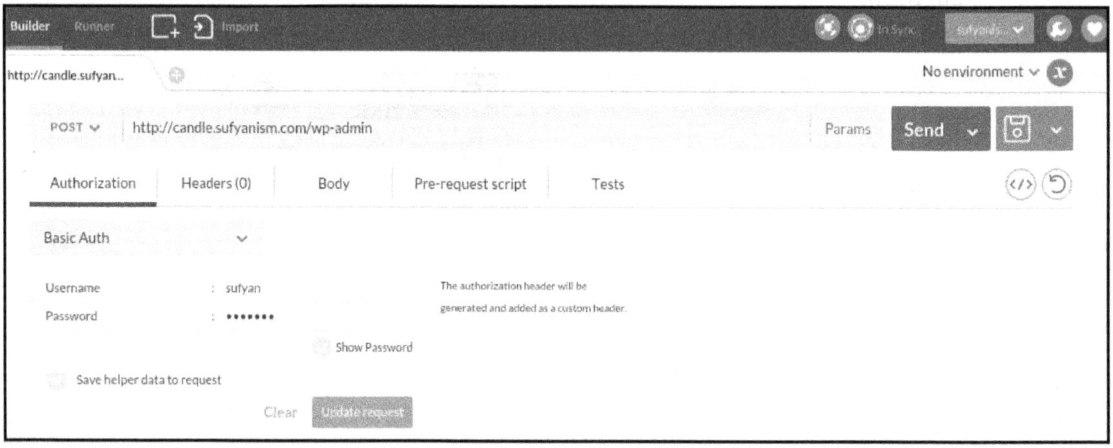

For all practical purposes, using Postman to authenticate you via HTTP requests is possible and feasible. However, since our focus is on the usage of REST API in WordPress, let us now get started with some actual code!

HTTP API in WordPress

As the name suggests, in WordPress, the HTTP API can be used to simplify HTTP requests. It can let you make HTTP requests via PHP, either to the same site or to a different site. But more importantly, HTTP API in WordPress lets you transform URL strings into JSON objects.

Consider the following URL string: `http://example.com/wp-json/wp/v2/posts`.

It is like any other URL on the Internet. Now, with HTTP API, we can convert it into a JSON object, making use of the `wp_remote_get ()` function from the WordPress core:

```
$json = wp_remote_get ( 'http://example.com/wp-json/wp/v2/posts' );
```

Now, `$json` will yield an array, and that is precisely the response that we need.

To understand it better, let us now put together a very small function that accepts a URL string and then gives an array of post objects:

```
$response = wp_remote_get( $url );
function get_json( $url ) {
//GET remote site
$response = wp_remote_get( $url );
//Checking for errors
if ( is_wp_error( $response ) ) {
return sprintf( 'Your URL %1s could not be retrieved', $url );
//GET only body
$data = wp_remote_retrieve_body( $response );
  }
//return if no error
if ( ! is_wp_error( $response ) ) {
//Now, decode and return
return json_decode( $response );
  }
}
```

What does the preceding code do? It makes a GET request and loads the URL string. To be sure that we are doing everything alright, we check whether our parameter is part of the `WP_Error` class or not because if it is, we have encountered an error. And if it is not, we can proceed with the JSON object.

Now, to test the preceding function, you can just pass any URL string for `$url`. Why not give it a shot and pass the URL to your test installation of WordPress, whatever it might be?

Ideally, the following is what your output should look like; it is pretty raw, but for a test code, this should show you that it works:


```
[{"id":1,"date":"2016-01-11T12:52:50","date_gmt":"2016-01-11T12:52:50","guid":{"rendered":"http:\/\
11T12:52:50","modified_gmt":"2016-01-11T12:52:50","slug":"hello-world","type":"post","link":"http:\
world!"},"content":{"rendered":"<p>Welcome to WordPress. This is your first post. Edit or delete it
WordPress. This is your first post. Edit or delete it, then start writing!
<\/p>\n"},"author":1,"featured_image":0,"comment_status":"open","ping_status":"open","sticky":false
[{"href":"http:\/\/candle.sufyanism.com\/wp-json\/wp\/v2\/posts\/1"}],"collection":[{"href":"http:\
[{"href":"http:\/\/candle.sufyanism.com\/wp-json\/wp\/v2\/types\/post"}],"author":[{"embeddable":tr
json\/wp\/v2\/users\/1"}],"replies":[{"embeddable":true,"href":"http:\/\/candle.sufyanism.com\/wp-j
[{"href":"http:\/\/candle.sufyanism.com\/wp-json\/wp\/v2\/posts\/1\/revisions"}],"https:\/\/api.w.o
json\/wp\/v2\/media?parent=1"}],"https:\/\/api.w.org\/term":[{"taxonomy":"category","embeddable":tr
json\/wp\/v2\/posts\/1\/categories"},{"taxonomy":"post_tag","embeddable":true,"href":"http:\/\/cand
{"taxonomy":"post_format","embeddable":true,"href":"http:\/\/candle.sufyanism.com\/wp-json\/wp\/v2\
[{"embeddable":true,"href":"http:\/\/candle.sufyanism.com\/wp-json\/wp\/v2\/posts\/1\/meta"}]}}]
```


Fetching GET post output in JSON objects

So far, we have seen how to GET posts and JSON objects. The preceding queries are sufficient to fetch (or GET) data for you, but how will you output the posts?

In WordPress, we often output posts by using the `get_post()` function that uses the global `$post` object. In a similar manner, we can use a loop that runs through all the posts retrieved by REST API and outputs them accordingly. For example, consider the following code:

```
$url = add_query_arg( 'per_page', 10, rest_url() );
$posts = get_json( $posts );
if ( ! empty( $posts ) ) {
  foreach( $posts as $post ) { ?>
  <article id="<?php echo esc_attr($post->ID ); ?>">
    <h1><?php echo $post->title; ?></h1>
    <div><?php wpautop( $post->content ); ?></div>

  </article>
<?php } //foreach
}
```

Looking at the outcome of this loop when used within a standard function, this is how it will work (the test site has, for example, a post called **Hello World!**):

As you can see, the preceding code is very easy to use and we can make use of REST API to return posts and output them accordingly. The preceding code is in PHP simply because WordPress is coded in PHP. If you are coming from another programming language, the logic behind the loop will remain the same, and on the basis of methods we have already discussed in the previous chapter, you can implement it accordingly.

Issuing queries

WordPress developers generally use the `WP_Query` parameters for fetching posts or issuing queries. When working with REST API in WordPress, we can still rely on a subset of `WP_Query` parameters in order to query our site or other sites.

Now, on the basis of our requirements, we will need to alter the filters and parameters accordingly. For example, you may wish to query the first *N* number of posts, or query on the basis of post title, or query on the basis of post status (published, draft, pending review, and so on).

Once more, assuming our WordPress site is hosted at `example.com` and we wish to query five posts in alphabetical order, the following is how our URL string might look like: `http://example.com/wp-json/wp/v2/posts?per_page=5&order=ASC`.

But do we really need to type out URLs? No we do not. WordPress has the `add_query_arg()` function that can automate the task for you. Now, if we were to pass the preceding condition or URL string to our function, the following is how it will look like:

```
$arg = array(
  'filter[orderby]' => 'title',
  'filter[per_page]' => 5,
  'filter[order]' => 'ASC'
);
$url = add_query_arg( $arg, rest_url( 'posts' ) );
```

It gets easier to use this function with jQuery's AJAX API, and we will discuss it in detail in a later chapter of this book.

Now, so far, you have learned how to issue basic queries in WordPress with REST API and have even worked with the default REST API routes in WordPress. Of course, you can make use of custom routes in REST API as well, but we shall save that discussion for a later chapter.

That said, in the previous examples, we have chosen to rely on the default post types in WordPress. What if you ever need to work with custom post types?

Basically, everything you can do with default post types in WordPress via REST API can be accomplished with custom post types as well. If you are registering or creating custom post types for your plugin or theme and you wish to add support for REST API for your custom post types, simply set the `show_in_rest` variable to `TRUE`. This will allow you to create routes and endpoints for REST API for that given custom post type.

On the other hand, if you wish to disallow usage of that custom post type via REST API, you can set the `show_in_rest` variable to `FALSE`.

That is all that you need to bear in mind with respect to custom post types. Everything else, in terms of routes and access permissions, remains the same as with default post types.

So far, you have learned how to issue basic requests in REST API over WordPress as well as how to work with request responses. However, since REST API is something that is generally used for *remote* access, you also need to know how to work between two different WordPress sites using REST API.

Therefore, in this section, our focus will now shift to cross-site interaction. We will learn how to copy posts from one site to another, as well as display and create posts on a remote site.

As you might have guessed by now, these actions will need POST requests and you will be passing JSON objects via these requests. In the previous section, we had setup functions for generating GET requests and URL strings. We will build upon our existing knowledge of those functions.

Interacting REST API via PHP

Let us now learn how to copy posts from one site to another site. Basically, we will be using REST API to GET JSON post data and convert it into a PHP object. In the previous section, we have already created a function for this and we will reuse the code. It is as simple as passing the following request:

```
$url = 'http://example.com/wp-json/wp/v2/posts/1';
$post = get_json( $url );
```

Now, to create a copy of the `post`, we just have to turn `$post` into an array and then pass it to `wp_insert_post()`.

To convert `$post`, we will follow a standard web development practice. Before the code, let us first spend some time understanding what we need to do.

Explanation of function

As already stated, we have to ensure that the data being passed to the function is an array. If the data is an object, we will need to typecast it as an array because the rest of the function will require an array.

Thereafter, once we have an array, we will setup a second array because we will be converting or copying the array keys. For instance, we will copy values from array key `X` to array key `post_X` and then unset the old key values.

Lastly, we just need to pass the array to `wp_insert_post()`. This function will create a new post for us and also return the ID of the new post.

Now that we know what we are trying to do, let us put it in practice. The following is what the code should look like:

```
function insert_post_from_json( $post ) {
//checking to see if array or object; because we can work only with array
if ( is_array( $post ) || ( is_object( $post ) && ! is_wp_error( $post ) )
) {
//ensure $post is an array; or force typecast
$post = (array) $post;
}
else {
return sprintf( '%1s must be an object or array', __FUNCTION__ );
}
//Create new array for conversion
//Set ID as post_id to try and use the same ID; note that leaving ID as ID
would //UPDATE an existing post of the same ID
$convert_keys = array(
     'title' => 'post_title',
     'content' => 'post_content',
     'slug' => 'post_name',
     'status' => 'post_status',
     'parent' => 'post_parent',
     'excerpt' => 'post_excerpt',
     'date' => 'post_date',
     'type' => 'post_type',
     'ID' => 'post_id',
);
//copy API response and unset old key
foreach ( $convert_keys as $from => $to ) {
if ( isset( $post[ $from ] ) ) {
    $post[ $to ] = $post[ $from ];
    unset( $post[ $from ] );
}
}
```

```
//remove all keys of $post that are disallowed and convert objects (if any)
to strings
$allowed = array_values( $convert_keys );
foreach( $post as $key => $value ) {
if( ! in_array( $key, $allowed ) ) {
unset( $post[ $key ] );
} else{
if ( is_object( $value ) ) {
$post[ $key ] = $value->rendered;
}
}
}
//All done. Create post and return its ID
return wp_insert_post( $post );
}
```

The output of our function will result in copying a post from a remote site to our site. You can see the new post, thereafter, on your WordPress site, as shown in the following screenshot:

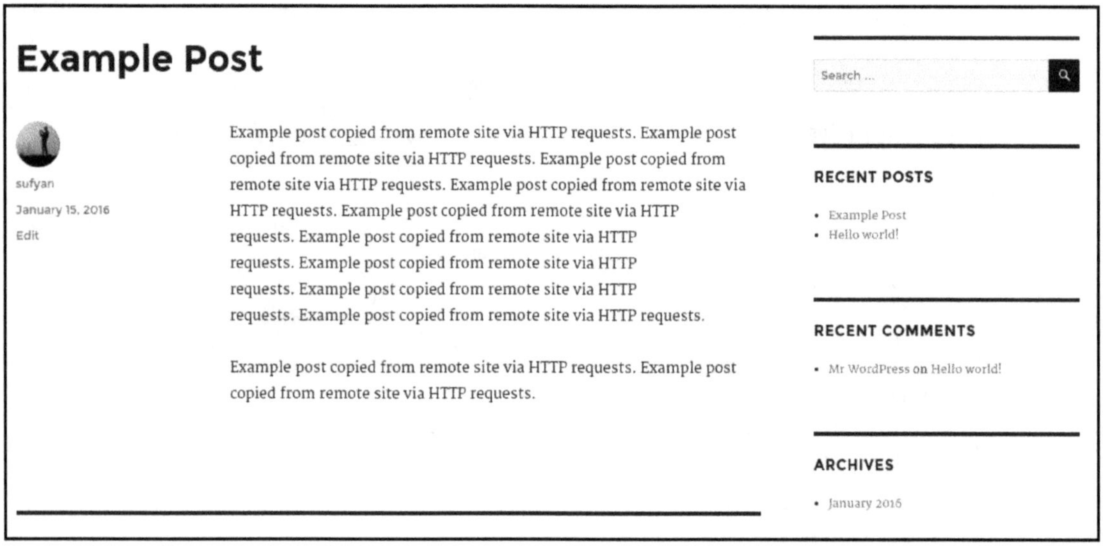

Issuing POST requests

So, in the previous section, we saw how to copy an existing post from a remote site to our site. However, what if we wish to create a new post directly? For that purpose, we will need to issue a POST request using the WordPress HTTP API.

We will be making use of the `wp_remote_post()` function that can be used to issue POST requests. As you might already be aware, if you have ever developed for WordPress, this function will ask you for two parameters: a URL to make the POST request and a corresponding array of arguments to pass along with your request. Once again, we will get an array and work with it, or if an array is not given, we will force typecast it to an array form.

To authorize the object, we will use a code that looks similar to the following:

```
$url = 'http://example.com/wp-json/wp/v2/posts/1';
$body = get_json( $url );
if ( is_object( $post ) ) {
  $body = $post;
  $headers = array (
    'Authorization' => 'Basic ' . base64_encode( 'admin' .       ':' .
'password' ),
  );
$remote_url = 'http://example-remote.com/wp-json/wp/v2/posts';
}
```

Here, the example `remote.com` is the remote site URL.

In the preceding code sample, we are first getting an object and then verifying if it truly is an object. Once verified, we just need to setup headers for authentication and provide the authentication details. Next, we are putting the URL for the endpoint of the post of the remote site in `$remote_url` so that we can actually make the POST request.

What next? We will carry on with the preceding code and send the request to `wp_remote_post()`, along with the required arguments as follows:

```
//Authentication
$url = 'http://example.com/wp-json/wp/v2/posts/1';
$body = get_json( $url );
if ( is_object( $post ) ) {
  $body = $post;
  $headers = array (
    'Authorization' => 'Basic ' . base64_encode( 'admin' .       ':' .
'password' ),
  );
$remote_url = 'http://example-remote.com/wp-json/wp/v2/posts';
```

```
}

$headers = array ('Authorization' => 'Basic ' . base64_encode( 'admin' .
':' . 'password' ),
  );

//Copying response
$response = wp_remote_post( $remote_url, array (
    'method'      => 'POST',
    'timeout'     => 45,
    'redirection' => 5,
    'httpversion' => '1.0',
    'blocking'    => true,
    'headers'     => $headers,
    'body'        => json_encode( $post ),
    'cookies'     => array ()
    )
  );

//Checking if error occurred.
if ( is_wp_error( $response ) ) {
  $error_message = $response->get_error_message();
  echo sprintf(  '<p>Error: %1s</p>', $error_message );
  }
else {
  echo 'Response:<pre>';
  print_r( $response );
  echo '</pre>';
  }
}
else {
  $error_message = 'Data invalid!';
  echo sprintf(  '<p>Error: %1s</p>', $error_message );
}
```

Once you run the preceding code, your remote site will return a success code in the header, meaning that the POST request completed successfully. For HTTP requests, **200OK** is the standard response that means everything went alright. If not, you will be presented with an error with details of that error.

On successful completion of the code request, the response code will look like as shown in the following screenshot:

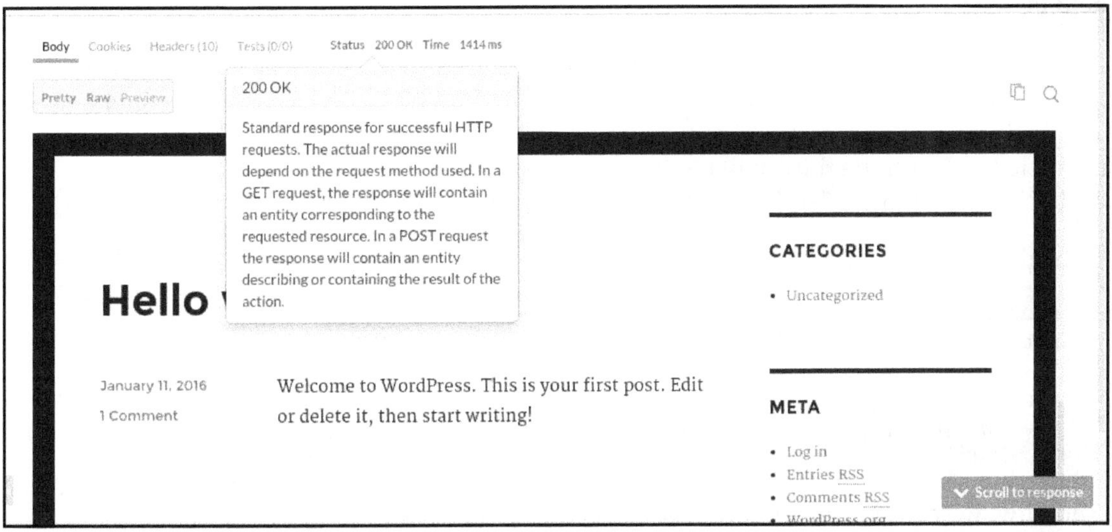

We will now turn our attention towards post meta fields in WordPress. Every WordPress developer is aware of the role of post metadata in development. However, how do we work with, retrieve, or update post metadata in WordPress using REST API? The following section will answer the question.

Also, note that while the following has been written with post metadata and meta fields in mind, the logic can easily be applied to user metadata and meta fields as well.

Implementing GET meta fields using REST API in WordPress

First up, let us start with GET requests. So far, we have been issuing GET requests to fetch posts via REST API. However, with such queries, the post meta fields are not included.

Now, in order to successfully GET post meta fields using REST API, we will need an endpoint with authentication.

Let us try to understand this with an example. Say, we have a post type called `painter`, and an associated meta field named `water_color`. Now, say we wish to pass a GET request to `wp-json/wp/v2/painter`, and with the results, we also want to GET the value held by the `water_color` field.

For this purpose, we can use the `register_api_field()` function that can add an extra meta field to the response. This function will require three arguments: the first, obviously, will be the post type for which we need to add the field for, the second will be the name of the meta field, and the third will be the array of arguments wherein you can define the callback method to GET or POST the value of the meta field.

To begin, let us set some callback methods:

```
function get_post_meta_clbk( $object, $field_name, $request ) {
return get_post_meta( $object[ 'id' ], $field_name );
}
function update_post_meta_clbk( $value, $object, $field_name ) {
return update_post_meta( $object[ 'id' ], $field_name, $value );
}
```

And now, we can simply register our API fields, as follows:

```
add_action( 'rest_api_init', function() {
register_api_field( 'painter',
'water_color',
array(
'get_callback'  => 'get_post_meta_clbk',
'update_callback' => 'update_post_meta_clbk',
'schema'  => null,
)
);
});
```

After this, each time you make a GET request to `wp-json/wp/v2/painter`, you will also be given the value of the corresponding meta field. The following is how it might look in the raw output:

```
"id":8,"date":"2016-01-15T19:21:09","date_gmt":"2016-01-15T19:21:09","guid":{"rendered":"http:\
5T19:21:09","modified_gmt":"2016-01-15T19:21:09","slug":"painter","type":"post","link":"http:\/
"rendered":"<p>This is the sample PAINTER post.\u00a0This is the sample PAINTER post.\u00a0This
\/p>\n"},"excerpt":{"rendered":"<p>This is the sample PAINTER post.\u00a0This is the sample PA
AINTER post.<\/p>\n"},"author":1,"featured_image":0,"comment_status":"open","ping_status":"oper
{"href":"http:\/\/candle.sufyanism.com\/wp-json\/wp\/v2\/posts\/8"}],"collection":[{"href":"htt
{"href":"http:\/\/candle.sufyanism.com\/wp-json\/wp\/v2\/types\/post"}],"author":[{"embeddable"
son\/wp\/v2\/users\/1"}],"replies":[{"embeddable":true,"href":"http:\/\/candle.sufyanism.com\/w
{"href":"http:\/\/candle.sufyanism.com\/wp-json\/wp\/v2\/posts\/8\/revisions"}],"https:\/\/api.
son\/wp\/v2\/media?parent=8"}],"https:\/\/api.w.org\/term":[{"taxonomy":"category","embeddable"
son\/wp\/v2\/posts\/8\/categories"},{"taxonomy":"post_tag","embeddable":true,"href":"http:\/\/c
"taxonomy":"post_format","embeddable":true,"href":"http:\/\/candle.sufyanism.com\/wp-json\/wp\/
{"embeddable":true,"href":"http:\/\/candle.sufyanism.com\/wp-json\/wp\/v2\/posts\/8\/meta"}]}}
```

And in the proper preview mode, it will look like the following:

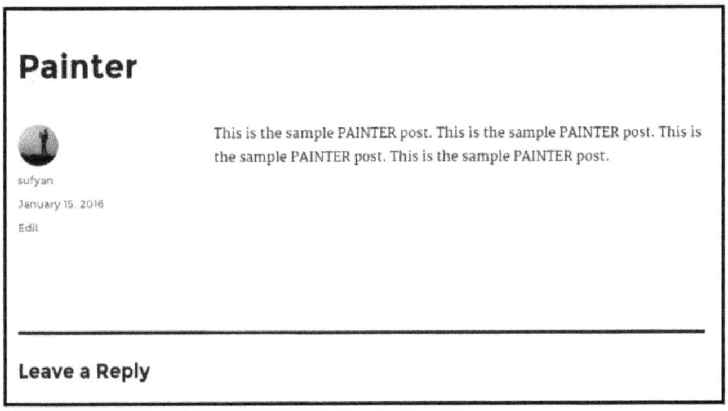

Note that the preceding GET requests will work only if the values of the meta fields are unprotected. For protected meta fields (in WordPress, they generally begin with an `underscore (_)`), the method is different, and we shall turn to that method now.

Implementing POST meta fields using REST API in WordPress

In our previous example, we saw how to get the value for the `water_color` field for a post type painter. Now, what if we wish to edit or create new value for that meta field?

Much like working without REST API, we need to find the meta ID for the given meta field and then pass that meta ID in order to tell WordPress that we wish to make changes or update the values for the concerned meta ID.

Thus, assuming that the meta ID is `10` for the post type ID `1`, we will pass the POST request as such: `wp-json/wp/v2/painter/01/meta/10`.

Now, we can create the meta field and then issue the relevant requests, as shown in the following code:

```
//GET URL request
$url = rest_url( 'wp/v2/posts/1/meta' );
//ADD basic headers for authentication
$headers = array (
'Authorization' => 'Basic ' . base64_encode( 'admin' . ':' . 'password' ),
```

```
);
//ADD meta value to body
$body = array(
'key' => 'water_color',
'value' => 'blue'
);
//POST request
$response = wp_remote_request( $url, array(
'method' => 'POST',
'headers' => $headers,
'body' => $body
  )
);
//if no error, we GET ID of meta key
$body = wp_remote_retrieve_body( $response );
if ( ! is_wp_error( $body ) ) {
$body = json_decode( $body );
$meta_id = $body->id;
echo $body->value;
if ( $meta_id ) {
    //ADD meta ID to URL
$url .= '/' . $meta_id;
    //SEND value
$body = array(
'value' => 'blue'
    );
$response = wp_remote_request( $url, array(
'method' => 'POST',
      )
    );
'headers' => $headers,
'body' => $body
//if no error, then echo the value
$body = wp_remote_retrieve_body( $response );
if ( ! is_wp_error( $body ) ) {
$body = json_decode( $body );
echo $body->value;
    }
  }
}
```

If the preceding code runs well, you will get status code `200`, which implies that all is fine with your HTTP request, as shown in the following screenshot:

What are we doing in the preceding code? We are issuing requests to get the meta field value, and then editing it and passing the updated value. Simple!

As you can see from the preceding example, we can use the `register_api_field()` function to work with meta fields and update any type of value we want. As you progress with REST API in WordPress, you will notice that it is one of the most crucial functions when working with REST API.

Summary

In this chapter, you covered a lot vis-à-vis REST API in WordPress. You have learnt how to issue GET and POST requests via HTTP to WordPress sites. Plus, you also learnt how to work with posts and post meta fields and metadata.

You also got an overview of the remote management abilities of REST API by learning how to copy posts from one site to another or how to create new or edit existing posts.

In the next chapter, we will go a step ahead and start with taxonomies and users. We know that taxonomies and users are important entities in WordPress and we will be using REST API to manage and work with both of these in the next chapter.

3

Working with Taxonomies and Users with REST API

In the previous chapter, you learned how to work with posts and post metadata in WordPress using REST API. With the help of HTTP queries and requests, you can now easily get posts, edit as well as delete posts, and also alter or modify the post metadata as per our needs and requirements.

Such knowledge is enough if you wish to manage basic operations with posts using REST API. But for bigger and proper development, such as themes, plugins, or applications powered via REST API in WordPress, you need to dig deeper and learn more about other WordPress concepts and how to work with them using REST API.

In this chapter, we will continue on our journey and now turn toward taxonomies and users. You will learn how to manage and handle taxonomies and users in WordPress with the help of REST API.

Working with taxonomies in WordPress using REST API

Any user of WordPress knows that WordPress has some public and private taxonomies that you can edit and work with. The public ones are category, tag, and `post_format`. Note that REST API is not yet ready to support private taxonomies, though it might soon be in the near future; so we will omit the discussion on private taxonomies here.

We will first begin with a basic introduction as to how to work with taxonomies in WordPress, followed by the usual GET and POST requests. Note that at this stage, it is being assumed that you have mastered the code in the previous chapter, as we will be reusing some code aspects from `Chapter 2`, *Interacting with REST API in WordPress*. Furthermore, a basic knowledge of JavaScript and jQuery will be useful, especially because nearly everything related to REST API in WordPress is modeled around JavaScript.

Basics

Working directly with taxonomies in WordPress is fairly easy, and there are two direct ways in which you can work with taxonomies. First, you can list the terms of a given taxonomy. Second, you can use taxonomy terms for a given post.

In the first case, say you have a category car, and you list all the posts associated with the given category. In the second case, you have a post with the tags blue, diesel, and wheels. You can list all the tags associated with this post. If you have ever set up a WordPress blog, you surely must have used categories and tags to sort your posts, or display in sidebar widgets, and so on.

HTTP requests

When working with REST API in WordPress, the concept remains the same. You can enlist taxonomies and the posts associated with them, or posts and the taxonomies associated with them. As always, you use GET requests to get data without modifying it, or POST requests if you wish to edit or alter or modify the taxonomies or the terms. For example, consider the following code that we have modified from the previous chapter:

```
$sites = wp_get_sites();
$the_list = arr();
foreach( $sites as $site ) {
$response = wp_remote_get( get_rest_url( $site->site_id,
'wp/v2/terms/categories' ) );
if ( ! is_wp_error( $response ) ) {
$terms = json_decode( wp_remote_retrieve_body( $response ) );
$term_list = arr();
foreach( $terms as $term ) {
$term_list[] = sprintf( '<li><a href="%1s">%2s</a></li>', esc_url(
$term->link
),$term->name );
    }
if ( ! empty( $term_list ) ) {
$site_info = get_blog_details( $site->site_id );
```

```
$term_list = sprintf( '<ul>%1s</ul>', implode( $term_list ) );
$the_list[] = sprintf( '<li><a href="%1s">%2s</a><ul>%3s</ul>', $site_info-
>siteurl, $site_info->blogname, $term_list );
    }
  }
}
if ( ! empty( $the_list ) ) {
echo sprintf( '<ul>%1s</ul>', implode( $the_list ) );
}
```

What does the preceding code do? Much like the previous chapter, we are using a function to make the request and then running a loop through a PHP object.

Note that the preceding code will work in a WordPress multisite only. If you wish to use it on a single site installation, modify it as follows:

```
$response = wp_remote_get( rest_url( 'wp/v2/terms/categories' ) );
if ( ! is_wp_error( $response ) ) {
$terms = json_decode( wp_remote_retrieve_body( $response ) );
$term_list = array();
foreach( $terms as $term ) {
$term_list[] = sprintf( '<li><a href="%1s">%2s</a></li>', esc_url(
$term->link
),$term->name );
  }
if ( ! empty( $term_list ) ) {
echo sprintf( '<ul>%1s</ul>', implode( $term_list ) );
  }
}
```

We have just replaced `get_rest_url()` with `rest_url()`. The raw output will be plain text like this:


```
[{"id":8,"date":"2016-01-15T19:21:09","date_gmt":"2016-01-15T19:21:09","guid":{"rend
15T19:21:09","modified_gmt":"2016-01-15T19:21:09","slug":"painter","type":"post","li
{"rendered":"Painter"},"content":{"rendered":"<p>This is the sample PAINTER post.\u0
the sample PAINTER post.<\/p>\n"},"excerpt":{"rendered":"<p>This is the sample PAINT
post.\u00a0This is the sample PAINTER post.
<\/p>\n"},"author":1,"featured_image":0,"comment_status":"open","ping_status":"open"
[{"href":"http:\/\/candle.sufyanism.com\/wp-json\/wp\/v2\/posts\/8"}],"collection":[
[{"href":"http:\/\/candle.sufyanism.com\/wp-json\/wp\/v2\/types\/post"}],"author":[{
json\/wp\/v2\/users\/1"}],"replies":[{"embeddable":true,"href":"http:\/\/candle.sufy
[{"href":"http:\/\/candle.sufyanism.com\/wp-json\/wp\/v2\/posts\/8\/revisions"}],"ht
json\/wp\/v2\/media?parent=8"}],"https:\/\/api.w.org\/term":[{"taxonomy":"category",
json\/wp\/v2\/posts\/8\/categories"},{"taxonomy":"post_tag","embeddable":true,"href"
json\/wp\/v2\/posts\/8\/tags"}],"https:\/\/api.w.org\/meta":[{"embeddable":true,"hre
{"id":6,"date":"2016-01-15T19:16:22","date_gmt":"2016-01-15T19:16:22","guid":{"rende
15T19:16:22","modified_gmt":"2016-01-15T19:16:22","slug":"example-post","type":"post
Post"},"content":{"rendered":"<p>Example post copied from remote site via HTTP reque
copied from remote site via HTTP requests.\u00a0Example post copied from remote site
requests.\u00a0Example post copied from remote site via HTTP requests.\u00a0Example
site via HTTP requests.\u00a0Example post copied from remote site via HTTP requests.
copied from remote site via HTTP requests.<\/p>\n"},"excerpt":{"rendered":"<p>Exampl
site via HTTP requests.\u00a0Example post copied from remote site via HTTP requests.
from remote site via HTTP requests.\u00a0Example post copied from remote site via HT
post copied from remote site via HTTP requests.\u00a0Example post copied from remote
requests.\u00a0Example post copied from remote site via HTTP requests.
```


The preceding code will perform multiple HTTP requests and database queries and will return the taxonomies as per request.

Implementing REST API and JavaScript with taxonomies

Now that we have covered how to perform HTTP requests and query our database using REST API, it is time to implement it. We will now be focusing on implementation of REST API and JavaScript with taxonomies in WordPress.

How to send GET requests for taxonomies

In WordPress, you can query for posts by taxonomy. Alternatively, you can also list terms in taxonomy for a given post.

It is fairly easy and is just a matter of few HTTP requests.

To get posts from a given category, we pass the parameter `category_name`. For example, for the category `sample`, we will pass the request as follows:

```
sample_url( 'wp/v2/posts?filter[category_name]=sample' );
```

Similarly, to get posts with a given tag, use the tag parameter. For example, for the tag `sampletag`, we will pass the following request:

```
sample_url( 'wp/v2/posts?filter[tag]=sampletag' );
```

And if you wish to query multiple taxonomies, you can combine them in the same request:

```
sample_url( 'wp/v2/posts?[category_name]=sample&filter[tag]=sampletag' );
```

As you can see, these are just basic URL strings that are being passed as GET requests to get posts with the given taxonomies in WordPress via REST API.

How to send POST requests for taxonomies

If you recall the previous chapter, we learned how to send POST requests for updating and creation of posts, as well as for working with post metadata. In terms of taxonomies too, the case is no different, and the logic is the same. However, unlike post metadata, taxonomies can exist independently of the post. For example, you can have a category with no posts under it and so on. Thus, you need to work with the ID of the taxonomy term, rather than the post ID, in order to send POST requests.

First, you can use a GET request to get the ID of the taxonomy terms that you want. The code is as follows:

```
//GET request
$url = rest_url( 'wp/v2/posts/1/terms/category' );
$response = wp_remote_request( $url, array(
     'method' => 'GET'
)
);
$body = wp_remote_retrieve_body( $response );
if ( ! is_wp_error( $body ) ) {
//Decoding
$terms = json_decode( $body );
$terms = array_combine( wp_list_pluck( $terms, 'slug' ), wp_list_pluck(
$terms, id ) );
}
```

In the preceding GET request, we are just getting the categories of the post ID 1. This will give us an array of associated terms.

Thereafter, by sending authenticated requests, we can list terms, create, delete, and so on, as shown in the following:

```
//Checking for the taxonomy terms
if ( isset( $terms[ 'example' ] ) ) {
//get term ID
$term_id = $terms['example'];
 //Adding ID to URL
$term_url = $url . '/' . $term_id;
//DELETE request
$headers = array(
'headers' => array(
'Authorization' => 'Basic ' . base64_encode( 'admin : password' ),
    )
  );
$response = wp_remote_request( $term_url,
    array(
'method' => 'DELETE',
'headers' => $headers
    )
  );
}
```

By using the preceding code, we can list taxonomy terms as well as update them. Of course, as you can see, it is a multistep process, as we first need to get the term ID and then work according to it. In WordPress, it is easier to accomplish such tasks via a combined function, so that you can keep related code in one place and you do not have to worry about different steps all the time.

Given in the following is a basic function that does all of the aforementioned tasks. It first checks for the taxonomy term and then uses the ID of that term to add it to a post (using a POST request), and if the taxonomy term does not exist, it creates and then adds it to the post. Output follows the code:

```
<?php
function add_term_to_post( $post_id, $taxonomy, $term_slug, $term_name,
$auth_header ) {
//First, finding post type and if post exists
$post_type = get_post_type( $post_id );
if ( false == $post_type ) {
    return;
  }
if ( 'post' == $post_type ) {
$post_type = 'posts';
```

```
    }
  $term_url = rest_url( 'wp/v2/terms/' . $taxonomy );
  //GET request for ID
  $response = wp_remote_request( $term_url,
      array(
    'method' => 'GET',
      )
    );
  $body = wp_remote_retrieve_body( $response );
  if ( ! is_wp_error( $body ) ) {
  $terms = json_decode( $body );
  if ( ! empty( $terms ) ) {
  $term_id = false;
  foreach ( $terms as $term ) {
    if ( $term->slug == $term_slug ) {
    $term_id = $term->id;
             break;
           }
         }
  //Auth headers for POST request
  $headers['Authorization'] = $auth_header;
  //If term doesn't exist, we create it
  if ( ! $term_id ) {
  //PUT term slug and name in request
  $body = array(
  'slug' => sanitize_title( $term_slug ),
  'name' => $term_name
       );
  //POST request
  $create_term_url = rest_url( 'wp/v2/terms/' . $taxonomy );
  //Create term
  $response = wp_remote_request( $create_term_url,
             array(
  'method'  => 'POST',
  'headers' => $headers,
  'body'    => $body,
            )
          );
  wp_die( print_r( $response ) );
    //Finding term ID
  $body = wp_remote_retrieve_body( $response );
  if ( ! is_wp_error( $body ) ) {
              $term = json_decode( $body );
  if ( is_object( $term ) && isset( $term->id ) ) {
  $term_id = $term->id;
              }
          }
        }
```

```
// Adding term ID to post
if ( $term_id ) {
// Create URL for request
$post_term_url = rest_url( 'wp/v2/' . $post_type . '/' . $post_id . '/
terms/' . $taxonomy . '/' . $term_id );
// POST request
$response = wp_remote_request( $post_term_url,
            array(
'method'  => 'POST',
'headers' => $headers
            )
          );
do_action( 'slug_post_term_update', $response, $post_id, $post_type,
$taxonomy, $term_slug )
          }
      }
      return $term_id;
   }
}
```

Upon successful completion, you can create a term and add it to the post, and if it already exists, update it accordingly.

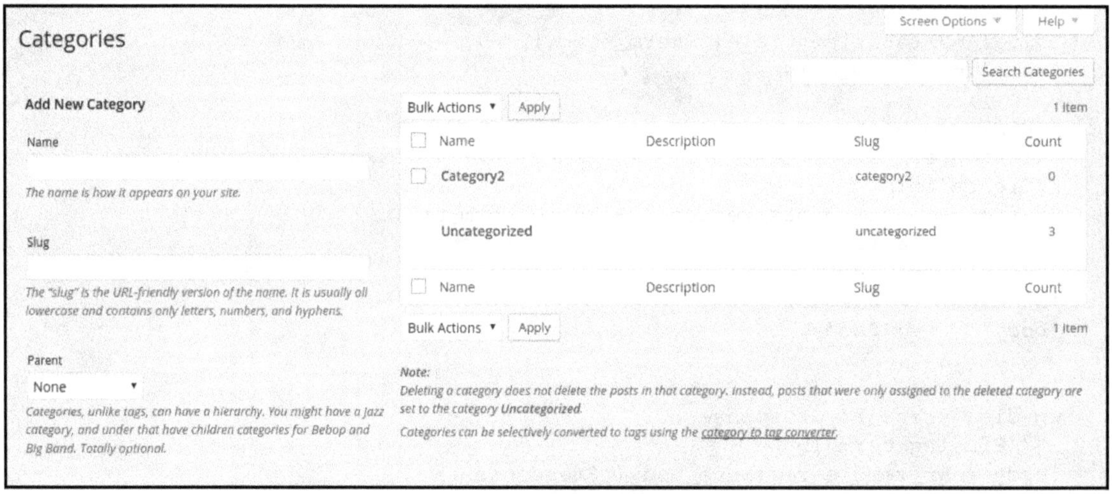

From this, we have learned how to send POST requests for taxonomies. The following will teach you how to work with users in WordPress by using REST API.

Working with users in WordPress using REST API

Now that we have learned how to work with taxonomies in WordPress using the REST API, it is time to turn our attention toward another useful concept-user management.

Since WordPress is a dynamic **content management system** that focuses also on blog management, the role of user accounts is pretty well-defined. You can have website administrators, editors, authors, contributors, and subscribers, each with their own set of privileges and access roles. Thus, while administrators can edit or tweak any aspect of your site, be it changing of themes or installation of plugins, authors can only work on their own posts, whereas subscribers can only read content or manage their profile.

So, what will we be covering in this section? Basically, we will learn how to create, edit, and work with user profiles using REST API. Starting now, there will not be much need for a detailed explanation, as the code is consistent in regard to how we treat data in WordPress using REST API. Thus, if you have followed the previous chapter and the previous section of this chapter and have learned how to work with and edit or modify posts, and post metadata and taxonomies in WordPress via REST API, user management too will be an easy task for you and won't require much rocket science.

How to GET user data using REST API in WordPress

Each user account in WordPress has two data types: `public` and `protected/privileged`. Public user data is that which can be browsed by users who are not logged in, whereas privileged data is that which only specific user accounts can access.

GET public user data

This is very simple to accomplish. Basically, with each post that can be viewed on your WordPress site (this includes all published posts, unless you protect them with a password or a custom plugin; this does not include draft posts or scheduled posts), there is some user data associated with it. Generally, it includes the post author's username, the URL of their author archive, author bio (if your active theme supports it), and user ID.

Now, you just need to make a proper GET request for the specific user and you can find the public user data easily.

For issuing a GET request for all the users with at least one published post, you can issue the GET request to `wp-json/wp/v2/users` of your WordPress site.

Why did I mention "at least one published post" in the preceding line? Because nonpublished posts cannot be accessed publicly.

However, for issuing a GET request for any specific user, you can use that user's user ID and pass it with your GET request. For instance, say if we wish to issue a GET request for a user with user ID `01`: `wp-json/wp/v2/users/01` is what it will look like.

And our output will be something like the following screenshot, in plain text and raw format:


```
{"id":1,"name":"sufyan","url":"","description":"","link":"http:\/\/candle.sufyanism.com\
{"24":"http:\/\/0.gravatar.com\/avatar\/9c3f6c90cca82f3cf2c3bd09baded08d?s=24&d=mm&r=g",
s=48&d=mm&r=g","96":"http:\/\/0.gravatar.com\/avatar\/9c3f6c90cca82f3cf2c3bd09baded08d?s
[{"href":"http:\/\/candle.sufyanism.com\/wp-json\/wp\/v2\/users\/1"}],"collection":[{"hr
```


Naturally, the preceding example is fairly basic and raw. However, you can use it in your REST API projects on WordPress to accomplish general fetch and GET requests for user accounts without authentication. Thus, even visitors who are not logged in can enlist and fetch such details with REST API.

GET privileged user data

You will need an authenticated request for privileged user data. If you are an administrator, everything is viewable to you, whereas for other user accounts, it depends on the type of user role and access rights that your account has.

Note that if you add a context set query parameter to your GET request, you can forcibly authenticate your request.

How to POST (and edit) user data using REST API in WordPress

If you are serious about using REST API in WordPress development, simple GET requests might not suffice for you, as you will also need to edit and update user accounts and user data.

The logic, once again, is simple here. The requests that we used previously, GET requests, can also be transformed as POST requests, when we wish to edit and update user data. However, unlike GET requests, POST requests require authentication, so you will need to pass the details such as username and password along with your request in order to verify your login and then edit or update the required user data accordingly.

Let us try to understand this with different code examples. First up, we shall create a new user with the help of a POST request to our WordPress website. We shall use jQuery to get the job done (for additional details about jQuery and JavaScript, be sure to refer to the final chapters of this book; since we are talking about WordPress development only, jQuery basics are beyond the scope of this book, but these have been covered at length in other Packt titles):

```
$.ajax( {
url: Slug_API_Settings.root + 'wp/v2/users/',
method: 'POST',
beforeSend: function ( xhr ) {
xhr.setRequestHeader( 'X-WP-Nonce', Slug_API_Settings.nonce );
},
data:{
email: 'test@example.com',
username: 'usertest',
password: Math.random().toString(46).substring(8)
}
} ).done( function ( response ) {
console.log( response );
} )
```

The preceding code will create a user with the username `usertest` and also assign a password.

If, however, you are using a different frontend than WordPress, you will need to authenticate yourself differently:

```
add_action( 'wp_enqueue_scripts', function() {
wp_enqueue_scripts( 'user-editor', plugin_dir_url( __FILE__ ) .'user-
editor.js', array('jquery')
);
```

```
wp_localize_scripts( 'user-editor', 'Slug_API_Settings', array(
'root' => esc_url_raw( rest_url() ),
'nonce' => wp_create_nonce( 'wp_rest' ),
'current_user_id' => (int) get_current_user_id()
) );
});
```

Both the preceding samples will create the user on your WordPress site.

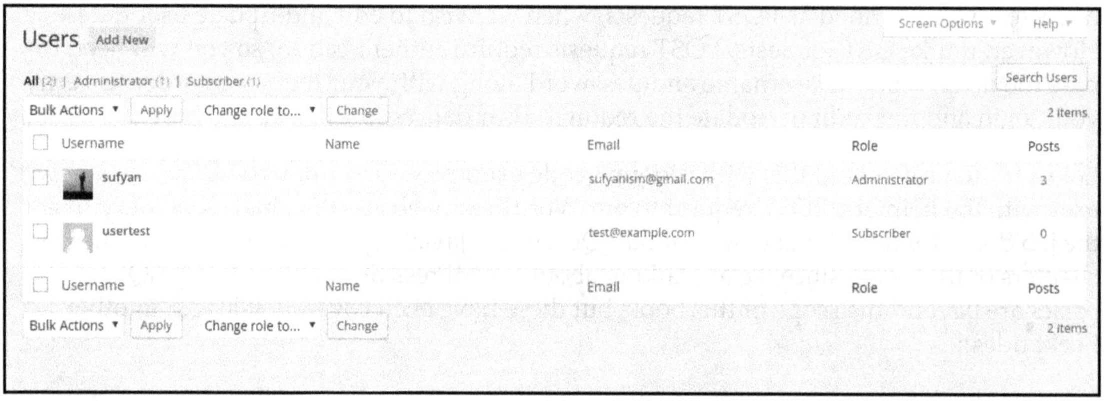

Note that the preceding samples require cookie-based authentication with a nonce check. In other words, you will need to be logged in as a user or administrator with sufficient privileges so as to be able to create a user account.

As you can see, by issuing the required requests, we can create user accounts in WordPress. Similarly, we can also update user data by pulling the required data and using a basic form for the update process.

To create the form, we use the following very basic HTML code:

```
<form id="profile-form">
<div id="username"></div>
<input type="text" name="email" id="email">
<input type="submit">
</form>
```

Then, we use a jQuery request to fetch the current user data and insert it in this form:

```
jQuery( document ).ready(function( $ ) {
$.ajax( {
url: Slug_API_Settings.root + 'wp/v2/users/' +
```

```
Slug_API_Settings.current_user_id + '?context=edit',
method: 'GET',
beforeSend: function ( xhr ) {
xhr.setRequestHeader( 'X-WP-Nonce', Slug_API_Settings.nonce );
}
} ).done( function ( user ) {
$( '#username' ).html( '<p>' + user.name + '</p>' );
$( '#email' ).val( user.email );
} );
});
```

The following is what it will look like once we have accomplished the task:

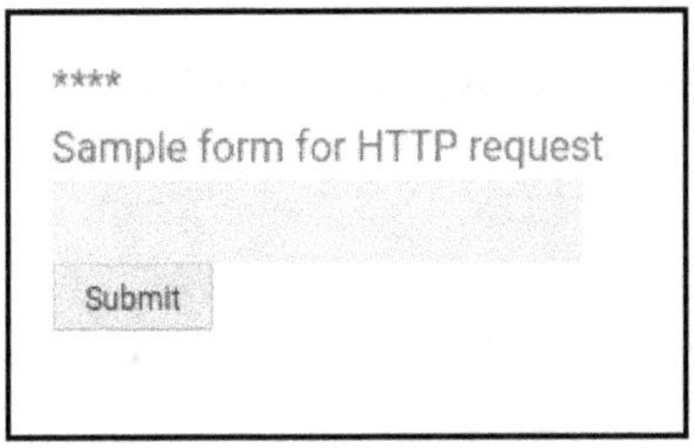

You might have noticed, in the preceding code, we are using a GET request, not a POST request. This is because we are just getting data, so a POST request is not required. Now, if we were to update the current user data, a POST request can be used. Again, for the similar structure and function, the following is what the POST request will look like in jQuery:

```
jQuery( document ).ready(function( $ ) {
var get_user_data;
(get_user_data = function () {
$.ajax( {
url: Slug_API_Settings.root + 'wp/v2/users/' +
Slug_API_Settings.current_user_id +
'?context=edit',
method: 'GET',
beforeSend: function ( xhr ) {
xhr.setRequestHeader( 'X-WP-Nonce', Slug_API_Settings.nonce );
}
} ).done( function ( user ) {
$( '#username' ).html( '<p>' + user.name + '</p>' );
$( '#email' ).val( user.email );
} );
})();
$( '#profile-form' ).on( 'submit', function(e) {
e.preventDefault();
$.ajax( {
```

```
url: Slug_API_Settings.root + 'wp/v2/users/' +
Slug_API_Settings.current_user_id,
method: 'POST',
beforeSend: function ( xhr ) {
xhr.setRequestHeader( 'X-WP-Nonce', Slug_API_Settings.nonce );
},
data:{
email: $( '#email' ).val()
}
} ).done( function ( response ) {
console.log( response )
} )
});
});
```

The output will be similar to the preceding cases, with the user fields being updated accordingly.

Summary

In this chapter, you learned how to work with users and taxonomies in WordPress with the help of REST API.

You can now send GET and POST requests to create, edit, and modify taxonomies. Similarly, you can also create and edit users on a WP site with such requests.

You also dealt with a fair bit of jQuery code in this chapter. In the following chapters, we will proceed toward working with AJAX and how to accomplish tasks, such as the processing of forms, in WordPress.

At this point, you can perform basic operations, and combined with the next few chapters, we will soon be able to create bigger applications and perform more complicated requests.

4
Working with Forms Using REST API

WordPress, being an ever-improving content management system, is now moving toward becoming a full-fledged application framework, which brings up the necessity for new APIs. The WordPress REST API has been created to create necessary and reliable APIs. The plugin provides an easy-to-use REST API, available via HTTP that grabs your site's data in the JSON format and further retrieves it.

WordPress REST API is now in its second version and has brought a few core differences, compared to the previous one, including route registration via functions, endpoints that take a single parameter, and all built-in endpoints that use a common controller.

Overview

In this chapter, you'll learn how to write a functional plugin to create and edit posts using the latest version of the WordPress REST API. This chapter will also cover the process on how to work efficiently with data to update your page dynamically based on results. This tutorial comes to serve as a basis and introduction to processing form data using REST API and AJAX and not as a redo of the WordPress post editor or a frontend editing plugin.

REST API's first task is to make your WordPress powered websites more dynamic, and for this precise reason, I have created a thorough tutorial that will take you step by step through this process. After you understand how the framework works, you will be able to implement it on your sites, thus making them more dynamic.

Fundamentals

As we start with our tutorial, it is very important to firstly focus on the previous chapters of this book and make sure you have fully understood your way through the process of creating posts by making POST requests to the posts endpoint. In this chapter, you will be doing something similar, but instead of using the WordPress HTTP API and PHP, you'll use jQuery's AJAX methods. All of the code for that project should go in its plugin file. Another important tip before starting is to have the required JavaScript client installed that uses the WordPress REST API. You will be using the JavaScript client to make it possible to authorize via the current user's cookies.

As a note for this tip would be the fact that you can actually substitute another authorization method such as OAuth if you find it more suitable.

Setting up the plugin

During the course of this tutorial, you'll only need one PHP and one JavaScript file. Nothing else is necessary for the creation of our plugin.

We will be starting off with writing a simple PHP file that will do the following three key things for us:

- Enqueue the JavaScript file
- Localize a dynamically created JavaScript object into the DOM when you use the said file
- Create the HTML markup for our future form

All that is required of us is to have two functions and two hooks. To get this done, we will be creating a new folder in our plugin directory with one of the PHP files inside it. This will serve as the foundation for our future plugin. We will give the file a conventional name, such as `my-rest-post-editor.php`.

In the following you can see our starting PHP file with the necessary empty functions that we will be expanding in the next steps:

```
<?php
/*
Plugin Name: My REST API Post Editor
*/
add_shortcode( 'My-Post-EditorR', 'my_rest_post_editor_form');
```

```
function my_rest_post_editor_form( ) {
}
add_action( 'wp_enqueue_scripts', 'my_rest_api_scripts' );
function my_rest_api_scripts() {
}
```

For this demonstration, notice that you're working only with the post title and post content. This means that in the form editor function, you only need the HTML for a simple form for those two fields.

Creating the form with HTML markup

As you will notice, we are only working with the post title and post content. This makes it necessary only to have the HTML for a simple form for those two fields in the editor form function. The necessary code excerpt is as follows:

```
function my_rest_post_editor_form( ) {
$form = '
<form id="editor">
<input type="text" name="title" id="title" value="My title">
<textarea id="content" ></textarea>
<input type="submit" value="Submit" id="submit">
</form>
<div id="results">
</div> ';
return $form;
}
```

Our aim is to show this only to those users who are logged in on the site and have the ability to edit posts. We will be wrapping the variable containing the form in some conditional checks that will allow us to fulfill the said aim. These tests will check whether the user is logged-in in the system or not, and if he's not, he will be provided with a link to the default WordPress login page.

The code excerpt with the required function is as follows:

```
function my_rest_post_editor_form( ) {
$form = '
<form id="editor">
<input type="text" name="title" id="title" value="My title">
<textarea id="content" ></textarea>
<input type="submit" value="Submit" id="submit">
</form>
<div id="results">
</div>
```

```
';
if (
is_user_logged_in() ) {
if ( user_can( get_current_user_id(), 'edit_posts' ) ) {
return $form;
}
else {
return __( 'You do not have permissions to do this.', 'my-rest-post-editor'
);
}
}
else {
    return sprintf( '<a href="%1s" >%2s</a>', wp_login_url( get_permalink(
get_
queried_object_id() ) ), __( 'You must be logged in to do this, please
click here to log in.',
'my-rest-post-editor') );
}
}
```

To avoid confusion, we do not want our page to be processed automatically or somehow cause a page reload upon submitting it, which is why our form will not have either a method or an action set. This is an important thing to notice because that's how we are avoiding the unnecessary automatic processes.

Enqueueing your JavaScript file

Another necessary thing to do is to enqueue your JavaScript file. This step is important because this function provides a systematic and organized way of loading JavaScript files and styles. Using the `wp_enqueue_script` function, you will tell WordPress when to load a script, where to load it, and what are its dependencies. By doing this, everyone utilizes the built-in JavaScript libraries that come bundled with WordPress rather than loading the same third-party script several times. Another big advantage of doing this is that it helps reduce the page load time and avoids potential code conflicts with other plugins.

We use this method instead of the wrong method of loading in the head section of our site because that's how we avoid loading two different plugins twice, in case we add one more manually.

Once the enqueuing is done, we will be localizing an array of data into it, which you'll need to include in the JavaScript that needs to be generated dynamically. This will include the base URL for the REST API, as that can change with a filter, mainly for security purposes.

Our next step is to make this piece as usable and user-friendly as possible, and for this, we will be creating both a failure and success message in an array so that our strings will be translation friendly. When this has been done, you'll need to know the current user's ID and include that one in the code as well.

The result we have accomplished so far is due to the `wp_enqueue_script()` and `wp_localize_script()` functions. It would also be possible to add custom styles to the editor, and that can be achieved by using the `wp_enqueue_style()` function.

While we have assessed the importance and functionality of `wp_enqueue_script()`, let's take a close look at the other ones as well.

The `wp_localize_script()` function allows you to localize a registered script with data for a JavaScript variable. By this, we will be offered a properly localized translation for any used string within our script. As WordPress currently offers a localization API in PHP; this comes as a necessary measure. Though the localization is the main use of the function, it can be used to make any data available to your script that you can usually only get from the server side of WordPress.

The `wp_enqueue_style` function is the best solution for adding stylesheets within your WordPress plugins, as this will handle all of the stylesheets that need to be added to the page and will do it in one place. If you have two plugins using the same stylesheet and both of them use the same handle, then WordPress will only add the stylesheet on the page once.

When adding things to `wp_enqueue_style`, it adds your styles to a list of stylesheets it needs to add on the page when it is loaded. If a handle already exists, it will not add a new stylesheet to the list. The function is as follows:

```
function my_rest_api_scripts() {
wp_enqueue_script( 'my-api-post-editor', plugins_url( 'my-api-post-
editor.js', __FILE__ ),
array( 'jquery' ), false, true );
wp_localize_script( 'my-api-post-editor', 'my_post_editor', array(
'root' => esc_url_raw( rest_url() ),
'nonce' => wp_create_nonce( 'wp_json' ),
'successMessage' => __( 'Post Creation Successful.', 'my-rest-post-editor'
),
'failureMessage' => __( 'An error has occurred.', 'my-rest-post-editor' ),
'userID'    => get_current_user_id(),
) );
}
```

That will be all the PHP you need as everything else is handled via JavaScript. Creating a new page with the editor shortcode (`MY-POST-EDITOR`) is what you should be doing next and then proceed to that new page. If you've followed the instructions precisely, then you should see the post editor form on that page. It will obviously not be functional just yet, not before we write some JavaScript that will add functionality to it.

Issuing requests for creating posts

To create posts from our form, we will need to use a POST request, which we can make by using jQuery's AJAX method. This should be a familiar and very simple process for you; however, if you're not familiar with it, you may want to take a look through the documentation and guidelines offered by the guys at jQuery themselves (`http://api.jquery.com/jquery.ajax/`). You will also need to create two things that may be new to you, such as the JSON array and the authorization header. In the following, we will be walking through each of them in details.

To create the JSON object for your AJAX request, you must firstly create a JavaScript array from the input and then use the `JSON.stringify()` to convert it into JSON. The `JSON.strinfiy()` method will convert a JavaScript value to a JSON string by replacing values if a replacer function is specified or optionally including only the specified properties if a replacer array is specified. The following code excerpt is the beginning of the JavaScript file that shows how to build the JSON array:

```
(function($){
$( '#editor' ).on( 'submit', function(e) {
        e.preventDefault();
var title = $( '#title' ).val();
var content = $( '#content' ).val();
        var JSONObj = {
"title"  :title,
"content_raw" :content,
"status"  :'publish'
};
        var data = JSON.stringify(JSONObj);
})(jQuery);
```

Before passing the variable data to the AJAX request, you will have first to set the URL for the request. This step is as simple as appending `wp.v2/posts` to the root URL for the API, which is accessible via `_POST_EDITOR.root`:

```
var url = _POST_EDITOR.root;
url = url + 'wp/v2/posts';
```

The AJAX request will look a lot like any other AJAX request you would make, with the sole exception of the authorization headers. Because of REST API's JavaScript client, the only thing that you will be required to do is to add a header to the request containing the nonce set in the `_POST_EDITOR` object. Another method that could work as an alternative would be the OAuth authorization method.

Nonce is an authorization method that generates a number for specific use, such as a session authentication. In this context, **nonce** stands for *number used once* or *number once*.

OAuth authorization method

OAuth authorization method provides users with secure access to server resources on behalf of a resource owner. It specifies a process for resource owners to authorize third-party access to their server resources without sharing any user credentials. It is important to state that it is has been designed to work with HTTP protocols, allowing an authorization server to issue access tokens to third-party clients. The third party would then use the access token to access the protected resources hosted on the server.

Using the `nonce` method to verify cookie authentication involves setting a request header with the name `X-WP-Nonce`, which will contain the said nonce value. You can then use the `beforeSend` function of the request to send the nonce. Following is what that looks like in the AJAX request:

```
$.ajax({
           type:"POST",
url: url,
dataType : 'json',
data: data,
           beforeSend : function( xhr ) {
               xhr.setRequestHeader( 'X-WP-Nonce', MY_POST_EDITOR.nonce );
},
});
```

As you might have noticed, the only missing things are the functions that would display success and failure. These alerts can be easily created by using the messages that we localized into the script earlier. We will now output the result of the provided request as a simple JSON array so that we can see what it looks like.

Following is the complete code for the JavaScript to create a post editor that can now create new posts:

```
(function($){
$( '#editor' ).on( 'submit', function(e) {
       e.preventDefault();
var title = $( '#title' ).val();
var content = $( '#content' ).val();
       var JSONObj = {
"title"   :title,
"content_raw" :content,
"status"   :'publish'
};
       var data = JSON.stringify(JSONObj);
       var url = MY_POST_EDITOR.root;
       url += 'wp/v2/posts';
       $.ajax({
           type:"POST",
           url: url,
           dataType : 'json',
           data: data,
           beforeSend : function( xhr ) {
               xhr.setRequestHeader( 'X-WP-Nonce', MY_POST_EDITOR.nonce );
},
success: function(response) {
               alert( MY_POST_EDITOR.successMessage );
               $( "#results").append( JSON.stringify( response ) );
},
failure: function( response ) {
               alert( MY_POST_EDITOR.failureMessage );
}
});
});
})(jQuery);
```

This is how we can create a basic editor in `WP REST API`.

If you are a logged in and the API is still active, you should create a new post and then create an alert telling you that the post has been created. The returned JSON object would then be placed into the `#results` container.

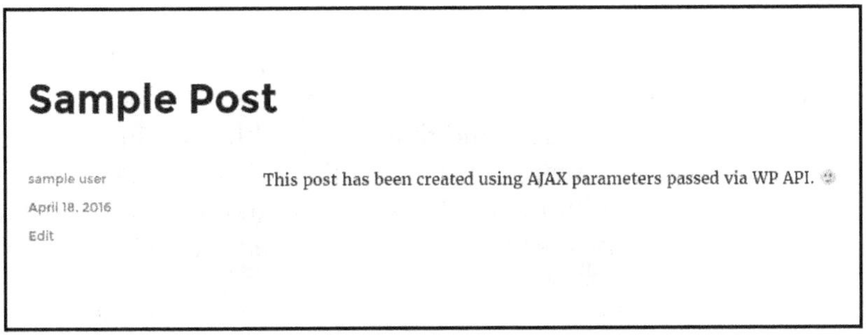

If you followed each and every step precisely, you should now have a basic editor ready. You may want to give it a try and see how it works for you. So far, we have created and set up a basic editor that allows you to create posts. In our next steps, we will go through the process of adding functionality to our plugin, which will enable us to edit existing posts.

Issuing requests for editing posts

In this section, we will go together through the process of adding functionality to our editor so that we can edit existing posts. This part may be a little bit more detailed, mainly because the first part of our tutorial covered the basics and setup of the editor.

To edit posts, we need to have the following two things:

- A list of posts by author, with all of the posts titles and post content
- A new form field to hold the ID of the post you're editing

As you can understand, the list of posts by author and the form field would lay the foundation for the functionality of editing posts.

Before adding that hidden field to your form, add the following HTML code:

```
<input type="hidden" name="post-id" id="post-id" value="">
```

In this step, we will need to get the value of the field for creating new posts. This will be achieved by writing a few lines of code in the JavaScript function. This code will then allow us to automatically change the URL, thus making it possible to edit the post of the said ID, rather than having to create a new one every time we go through the process.

This can be easily achieved by writing down a simple code piece, like the following one:

```
var postID = $( '#post-id').val();
if ( undefined !== postID ) {
url += '/';
   url += postID;
}
```

As we move on, the preceding code will be placed before the AJAX section of the editor form processor. It is important to understand that the variable URL in the AJAX function will have the ID of the post that you are editing only if the field has a value as well. The case in which no such value is present for the field, it will yield in the creation of a new post, which would be identical to the process you have been taken through previously.

It is important to understand that to populate the said field, including the post title and post content field, you will be required to add a second form. This will result in all posts being retrieved by the current user, by using a GET request. Based on the selection provided in the said form, you can set the editor form to update. In the PHP, you will then add the second form, which will look similar to the following:

```
<form id="select-post">
<select id="posts" name="posts">
</select>
<input type="submit" value="Select a Post to edit" id="choose-post">
</form>
```

REST API will now be used to populate the options within the `#posts` select. For us to achieve that, we will have to create a request for posts by the current user. To accomplish our goal, we will be using the available results. At this point, we are nearly finished with our tutorial, but you might want to go back to `Chapter 1`, *Getting Started with REST API,* and do a review on how to make GET requests to the REST API using PHP.

We will now have to form the URL for requesting posts by the current user, which will happen if you will set the current user ID as a part of the `_POST_EDITOR` object during the processes of the script setup.

A function needs to be created to get posts by the current author and populate the select field. This is very similar to what we did when we made our posts update, yet it is way simpler. This function will not require any authentication, and given the fact that you have already been taken through the process of creating a similar function, creating this one shouldn't be any more of a hassle for you.

The success function loops through the results and adds them to the post selector form as options for its one field and will generate a similar code, something like the following:

```
function getPostsByUser( defaultID ) {
   url += '?filter[author]=';
   url += my_POST_EDITOR.userID;
   url += '&filter[per_page]=20';
   $.ajax({
type:"GET",
url: url,
dataType : 'json',
success: function(response) {
var posts = {};
$.each(response, function(i, val) {
               $( "#posts" ).append(new Option( val.title, val.ID ) );
});
           if ( undefined != defaultID ) {
               $('[name=posts]').val( defaultID )
}
}
});
}
```

You will notice that the function we have created has one of the parameters set for `defaultID`, but this shouldn't be a matter of concern for you just now. The parameter, if defined, would be used to set the default value of the select field, yet, for now, we will ignore it. We will use the very same function, but without the default value, and will then set it to run on document ready. This is simply achieved by a small piece of code like the following:

```
$( document ).ready( function()
{
   getPostsByUser();
});
```

Having a list of posts by the current user isn't enough, and you will have to get the title and the content of the selected post and push it into the form for further editing.

This will ensure editing is done correctly and make it possible to achieve the projected result. Moving on, we will need the other GET request to run on the submission of the post selector form.

This should be similar to the following:

```
$( '#select-post' ).on( 'submit', function(e) {
   e.preventDefault();
   var ID = $( '#posts' ).val();
```

```
        var postURL = MY_POST_EDITOR.root;
        postURL += 'wp/v2/posts/';
        postURL += ID;
        $.ajax({
    type:"GET",
    url: postURL,
    dataType : 'json',
    success: function(post) {
    var title = post.title;
    var content = post.content;
              var postID = postID;
    $( '#editor #title').val( title );
    $( '#editor #content').val( content );
              $( '#select-post #posts').val( postID );
    }
    });
    });
```

In the form of `<json-url>wp/v2/posts/<post-id>`, we will build a new URL that will be used to scrape post data for any selected post. This will result in us making an actual request that will be used to take the returned data and then set it as the value of any of the three fields there in the editor form.

Upon refreshing the page, you will be able to see all posts by the current user in a specific selector. Submitting the data by a *click* will result in the following:

- The content and title of the post that you have selected will be visible to the editor, provided that you have followed the preceding steps correctly.
- The hidden field for the post ID you have added should now be set.

Even though the content and title of the post will be visible, we would still be unable to edit the actual posts as the function for the editor form was not set for this specific purpose, just yet. To achieve that, we will need to make a small modification to the function that will make it possible for the content to be editable. Besides, at the moment, we would only get our content and title displayed in raw JSON data; however, applying the method described previously will improve the success function for that request so that the title and content of the post displays in the proper container, `#results`. In order to achieve this, you will need a function that is going to update the said container with the appropriate data. The code piece for this function will be something like the following:

```
    function results( val ) {
    $( "#results").empty();
          $( "#results" ).append( '<div class="post-title">' + val.title +
    '</div>'  );
          $( "#results" ).append( '<div class="post-content">' + val.content +
```

```
'</div>'  );
}
```

The preceding code makes use of some very simple jQuery techniques, but it is still sufficient in providing a proper introduction to updating page content by making use of data from REST API. There are countless ways of getting a lot more detailed or creative with this if you dive in the markup or start adding any additional fields. That will always be an option for you if you're more of a savvy developer, but as an introductory tutorial, we're trying not to keep this tutorial extremely technical, which is why we'll stick to the provided example for now.

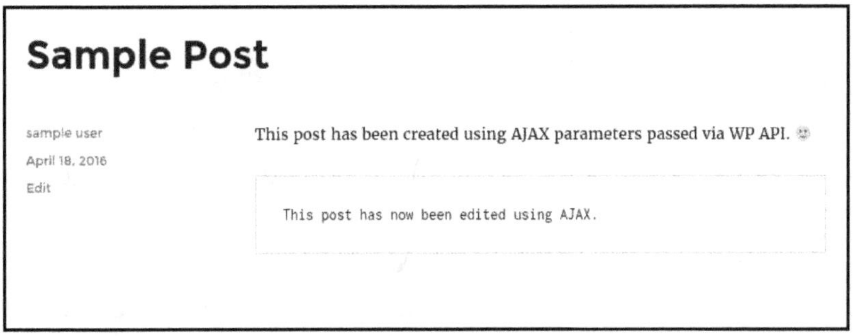

As we move forward, you can use it in your modified form procession function, which will be something like the following:

```
$( '#editor' ).on( 'submit', function(e) {
   e.preventDefault();
var title = $( '#title' ).val();
var content = $( '#content' ).val();
console.log( content );
   var JSONObj = {
"title"
"content_raw"
"status"
};
:title,
:content,
:'publish'
   var data = JSON.stringify(JSONObj);
   var postID = $( '#post-id').val();
   if ( undefined !== postID ) {
url += '/';
       url += postID;
}
   $.ajax({
```

```
        type:"POST",
url: url,
dataType : 'json',
data: data,
        beforeSend : function( xhr ) {
            xhr.setRequestHeader( 'X-WP-Nonce', MY_POST_EDITOR.nonce );
},
success: function(response) {
            alert( MY_POST_EDITOR.successMessage );
            getPostsByUser( response.ID );
results( response );
},
failure: function( response ) {
            alert( MY_POST_EDITOR.failureMessage );
}
});
});
```

As you will have noticed, a few changes have been applied, and we will go through each of them in specific detail:

- The first thing that has changed is the Post ID that's being edited is now conditionally added. This implies that we will make use of the form and it will serve to create new posts by POSTing to the endpoint. Another change with the POST ID is that it will now update posts via `posts/<post-id>`.
- The second change regards the success function. A new `result()` function was used to output the post title and content during the process of editing. Another thing is that we also reran the `getPostsbyUser()` function, yet it has been set in a way that posts will automatically offer the functionality of editing, just after you create them.

Summary

With this, we have completed this chapter, and if you have followed each step with precision, you should now have a simple yet functional plugin that can create and edit posts by using the WordPress REST API.

This chapter also covered techniques on how to work with data in order to update your page dynamically based on the available results. We will now progress toward further complicated actions with REST API.

5
Custom Routes in WordPress REST API

WordPress REST API, being treated as a consistent API, is mainly concerns the process of querying the default routes. One similar example that could be brought up is the Twitter API. It is important to set that WordPress REST API is made of a bunch of highly customizable APIs that could further be used as tools for creating a more extensive list of APIs.

Another key point to be mentioned in this regard is the fact that REST API is nothing like the core API, just as WordPress isn't all about the global `WP_Query` object. It is important to understand that we will go beyond the basics with our REST API project. While usual and more or less primitive projects may be successfully fulfilled without much hassle or usage of advanced techniques, you can't always go far with the basic techniques of REST API.

Another point is that the basic techniques are what the majority of sites will be based upon, which is why we can consider some default routes as a compromise between a huge amount amount of websites, including several ones that have not even been built yet.

Another example that would support this argument is the fact that sticking to defaults is like working on a common WordPress project without overwriting the default query at `pre_get_posts` or having any of your own `WP_Query` objects.

Overview

In this chapter, we will go through the process of developing a custom route with two endpoints that will display information regarding products on an e-commerce website. Of course, the e-commerce part is just an example, and you can very well use this model to display posts on a blog, photos from a portfolio site, and so on.

REST API, being in its second version, is split into two parts: the infrastructure for setting up RESTful APIs and a part covering the default routes that would work as fantastic examples that can guide you through creating your very own routes. The system used for adding these routes and endpoints is amazingly well set.

In this chapter, we will be exposing the specific custom fields that will be used on the site. In this implementation, a second route called docs will be incorporated, which will be set around a custom post type that we are using for documentation purposes. We want to make this as clear and thorough as possible, which is why our endpoints and routes are used for explanatory reasons.

Adding custom routes to WordPress REST API

In the second version of REST API, there is a new function called `register_rest_route()` that deserves our attention. It lets you add a route to REST API and then further pass it to an array of endpoints. For each endpoint provided, a defined value for each field will be given in our query, including defaults, validation and callbacks, sanitation, and separate permissions callback.

The focus will be put on the following three main key points:

- Callback
- Field arguments
- Permissions check

They will provide us with an idea on how the architectural side of the API functions. It is important to note that you will know that your requests are authorized, and your fields sanitized, and everything is in place once we get to our callback. This very same architectural structure is what will enforce separation of concerns and help maintain your code modular.

Setting up the custom route

We will be using the `register_rest_route()` function for defining a custom route in a function that will be then hooked up to the `rest_api_init` action, which will run upon the initialization of REST API. It will be equally important for an action, just like `init` and `plugin_loaded` are.

This function will accept the following four arguments:

- Route namespace
- URL after namespace
- Endpoints to a route
- Optional Boolean argument

We will look into the four arguments briefly as follows.

Route namespace

The first argument would the namespace for the route. It is important to understand that each and every route must be namespaced, which will further be used after the `wp-JSON` as the next URL segment. All default routes are namespaced with `wp`. Every core route will have URLs like `wp-JSON/wp/posts`, while custom route *colors* within the `my-shirt-shop` namespace will have the attribute URL as `wp-JSON/my-shirt-shop/colors`.

Those acting like PHP namespaces or unique slugs as functions for a plugin will work as the mean that is going to avoid clashes between routes. As you write, a plugin that adds a route called **menus** will be used side by side with another plugin that adds a route called menus, as long as namespaces that are different will further correspond to a plugin's name. Another point is that namespaces for routes will be a common system, which will be helpful, mainly because the chance is pretty high that several developers will use routes with similar names.

URL after namespace

Another argument is that the URL after the namespace for your route, being the second route, will allow for a number like a post ID in the last segment of the URL. Our first route in this example is /products and the second one is /products' . '/(?P<id>[\d]+). Our second route URL will get joined to the namespace. Your URL will go to something like /wp-JSON/Packt-API/products as long as your route is set as /products and then the namespace will be Packt-API. A tip for you would be to include the version number within your namespaces as that is considered to be a good practice:

```
register_rest_route( 'Packt-api', '/products', array() );
```

Endpoints to a route

We will be discussing endpoints to routes in detail later on, rather than here itself. This is because endpoints are very important in custom and default routes and deserve a separate discussion of their own. Therefore, we will continue the talk on this topic further.

Optional Boolean argument

The argument that should set our final ideas on this matter would be the override, also called an optional Boolean argument. The clashes that may occur with our already defined routes, whether they are intentional or unintentional, should be dealt by the override. The argument is usually set by default as false, and when this is the case, attempts to merge the routes will be made. Alternatively, you can set them to true and replace already declared routes.

Setting up the custom endpoints

We will now move on with some practical work, which will consist of us setting up our endpoints. As we have previously stated, routes would only be useful if they have endpoints, which is why the rest of this chapter will only cover the process of adding endpoints to the route using our third argument of register_rest_route().

Transport method

The transport method involves endpoints that need to define one or more HTTP transport methods, such as **DELETE**, **POST**, **PUT**, and **GET**. With an endpoint that is defined as working via a GET request, the REST API will receive the correct data and the way to create errors for invalid requests.

The array that defines your endpoint will further define the transport methods in a key named method. The following code example will provide you with the method of defining an endpoint that is going to allow only for GET requests and will underline the process on how the `WP_REST_Server` class provides constants for defining transport methods and types of JSON bodies to the request:

```
register_rest_route( 'Packt-api', '/products', array(

'methods'           => WP_REST_Server::READABLE,
) );
```

This is the way you would add a route that is going to accept all transport methods:

```
register_rest_route( 'Packt-api', '/products', array(

'methods'           => WP_REST_Server::ALLMETHODS,
) );
```

By making use of these constants, it is assured that the REST server will evolve and your routes will be properly set up and ready for it.

Defining our fields

The specification of the fields will regard what their defaults are and the method of sanitizing them which is something that's going to be helpful for us when we are about to define our endpoints. The callback function will then be allowed to process the request to trust the data that it is going to retrieve. The REST API will then handle everything for you, just like per the example, including the collection of products that will return the main field endpoint:

```
register_rest_route( "{$root}/{$version}", '/products', array(
    array(
'methods'           => \WP_REST_Server::READABLE,
'callback'          => array( $cb_class, 'get_items' ),
'args'              => array(
'per_page' => array(
'default' => 10,
```

```
'sanitize_callback' => 'absint',
        ),
'page' => array(
'default' => 1,
'sanitize_callback' => 'absint',
        ),
'soon' => array(
'default' => 0,
'sanitize_callback' => 'absint',
        ),
'slug' => array(
'default' => false,
'sanitize_callback' => 'sanitize_title',
        )
      ),
    ),
  )
'permission_callback' => array( $this, 'permissions_check' )
);
```

If you take a closer look, you will notice that most of these are actually Boolean fields or numbers. The purpose of them being set up this way is that they will be sanitized by using the `absint()` field. The `sanitize_title` field that is used for querying the post slug will follow the same process of sanitization before being written to the database.

The other route is used for displaying the product by its ID. In this route's endpoint, we have not specified any fields. Why have we not done so? Well, the logic behind not specifying any fields to this endpoint is simple; we just need to pass the ID in the last URL segment, and that will be enough for our goal. Another point is that we are not trying to over-complicate this process, so while we are still getting into technical details, the boredom or deep technicality will be avoided when possible:

```
register_rest_route( "{$root}/{$version}", '/products' . '/(?P<id>[\d]+)',
array(
array(
          'methods'            => \WP_REST_Server::READABLE,
          'callback'           => array( $cb_class, 'get_item' ),
          'args'               => array(
),
          'permission_callback' => array( $this, 'permissions_check' )
),
)
);
```

The examples provided can be easily used for crafting our routes, and all you have to do is remember that they were written in an object context, meaning that they are going to be used inside a method of class, which brings up the necessity for them to be attached to the `rest_api_init` action.

The callback function

As a reminder, I would like to reiterate that functions are first-class objects that we then further pass a function through, something like an argument in a different function that is later executed then passed into a function or even returned for its later execution. This is the purpose of using callback functions, which are probably the most widely used in functional programming, this technique being found in nearly every piece of jQuery or JavaScript coding.

The request that will be dispatched if the permissions callback passes is manifested for each route in the key, and the callback function specifically. In our previous example, the main route has been passed to a method of the callback class named `get_items`, whose single product route to a method called `get_item` was used. The callback class extents the class in the core API, `WP_REST_Post_Controller`, which later allows us to absorb a lot of its functionality while providing us with the possibility to use our routes. This also follows the conventions set out in the core post query class.

The permissions callback

Our authentication scheme makes use of parts of the request, and similar to the main callback, the permissions callback is passed by an object of `WP_Request_Class`. The permissions callback will just return either `true` or `false` results, and it's totally up to you how you get there. The method we will be using here is to make use of the traditional check of our current user capabilities logic that is used during WordPress development. The permissions check will then run after the user is set and our use of any of the authentication methods will be already run.

What we will do is add a specific authorization for our custom routes and check the specific parts of the request for the corresponding right keys, thus avoiding any reliance on WordPress' authentication or current user.

If there are social logins implemented on your site, you could try and perform checks for the OAuth keys and then authenticate them against that network. If they pass, you would then login with the user who's account is directly associated with the said account. This is just one of the strategies that we will be covering more thoroughly in future.

In our example here, we will go through the path of creating a read-only API that is public, which we could then either create a function that always returns `true` to use as our permissions callback or to use the `_return_true` that is available in WordPress. We went with the first option as it will be a necessity for our subsequent steps when the authenticated POST requests are added.

Processing requests (and responses)

The `WP_REST_Request` class will receive as an object the callback function of each endpoint, which will then further be passed as an object. To receive the parameters from the request, which are mapped from any transport method provided, we will be using the efficient method of `get_params()` to get all the data from the validated and sanitized request, with all of the correspondent defaults filled in. Instead of using the method of accessing the global GET or POST variables, we will be using the method described previously, and the reasons for that are the following:

- The array that is returned is validated and sanitized and will handle the switches between the transport method. Even if we choose to switch the endpoints definition from GET to PUT, which is a one—line change, then the code will suffer no consequences and will be functional and will as expected.
- Better abstraction is also acquired by using this method. Even within our basic version of the API add-on plugin that is used in this chapter—the source code for the plugin it is based on—the queries for the products' and docs' endpoints would still be handled by an abstract class that then further handles the creation of `WP_Query` arguments by looping through the available results and then returning them.

I hope we have assessed the importance and functionality of the method we have chosen to go with, and as that was set, it is important to understand our final necessity, which is the need to end with an instance of the `WP_REST_Response` class. Our best way of achieving that is by using the `ensure_rest_response()` function, which would then further return an instance of this class, which can also handle errors well.

The following class will ensure that our response is a properly formed JSON with the minimum amount of headers necessary while also providing methods for adding extra headers.

In the following example, you can see how it was used to add headers based on the core post routes and headers for the total results, pages and links like `prev/next`:

```
protected function create_resp( $reqst, $argz, $data ) {
$response
= rest_ensure_response( $data );
   $count_query = new \WP_Query();
   unset( $argz['paged'] );
   $query_result = $count_query->query( $argz );
   $total_posts  = $count_query->found_posts;
   $response->header( 'X-WP-Total', (int) $total_posts );
   $max_pages = ceil( $total_posts / $reqst['per_page'] );
   $response->header( 'X-WP-TotalPages', (int) $max_pages );
   if ( $reqst['page'] > 1 ) {
      $prev_page = $reqst['page'] - 1;
      if ( $prev_page > $max_pages ) {
         $prev_page = $max_pages;
}
      $prev_link = add_query_arg( 'page', $prev_page, rest_url( $this->base
) );
      $response->link_header( 'prev', $prev_link );
}
   if ( $max_pages > $reqst['page'] ) {
      $next_page = $reqst['page'] + 1;
      $next_link = add_query_arg( 'page', $next_page, rest_url( $this->base
) );
      $response->link_header( 'next', $next_link );
}
return $response;
}
```

While in this tutorial we are trying to assess quite a few technical methods, it's solely up to you how you want to get your data together for the response. Because the API and the project are solely yours, you have the availability of using any of the following methods, which I will briefly go through.

WP_Query

`WP_Query` is a defined class that deals with the intricacies of a page or post request sent to a WordPress blog. It is mainly used in one of the following two scenarios. The first is when you find out what type of request WordPress is currently dealing with. The second and more common scenario is when plugin developers use the `WP_Query` class in their loops to provide numerous functions for common tasks within it.

WPDB

WordPress defines a class named `WPDB`, which contains within itself some functions that are further used for the interaction with one of the databases, whose primary purpose is to provide an interface with the WordPress database that can be used to communicate with any other corresponding database.

get_post_meta

The `get_post_meta` function will be used to retrieve post meta field for a post that will be an array if the return is `false` or will be a value of the `meta_data` field if the return is `true`.

Third-party plugins

This one is a pretty obvious method, and it would suppose that you will rely on the functions that would then be part of a third-party plugin and its built-in functions.

Moving on from the method you will be using, we will recall the fact that you should already have classes for getting the required data if you're adding a RESTful API to any of the existing plugins or websites.

The REST API could then be used to get parameters for those classes from an HTTP request, which would then pass the results to the response class of the very same REST API. Within our example, in the API, we have used the `WP_Query` function to get the posts and the following provide the code piece for the method we used to loop through the `WP_Query` object and get the data we need:

```
protected function perform_query( $reqst, $argz, $respond = true) {
   $posts_query  = new \WP_Query();
   $query_result = $posts_query->query( $argz );
   $data = array();
if ( ! empty( $query_result ) ) {
foreach ( $query_result as $post ) {
          $image = get_post_thumbnail_id( $post->ID );
if ( $image ) {
$_image = wp_get_attachment_image_src( $image, 'large' );
if ( is_array( $_image ) ) {
                $image = $_image[0];
}
}
          $data[ $post->ID ] =
```

```
            'name'          =>
            'link'          =>
            'image_markup' =>
            'image_src'    =>
            'excerpt'      =>
            'tagline'      =>
            'price'       =>
            'slug'         =>
);
array(
$post->post_title,
get_the_permalink( $post->ID ),
get_the_post_thumbnail( $post->ID, 'large' ),
$image,
$post->post_excerpt,
get_post_meta( $post->ID, 'product_tagline', true ),
edd_get_variable_price( $post->ID ),
$post->post_name,
         for ( $i = 1; $i <= 3; $i++ ) {
foreach( array(
               'title',
               'text',
               'image'
            ) as $field ) {
               if ( 'image' != $field ) {
                  $field                          = "sample_{$i}_{$field}";
                  $data[ $post->ID ][ $field ] = get_post_meta( $post->ID,
$field, true );
}else{
                  $field                          = "sample_{$i}_{$field}";
                  $_field = get_post_meta( $post->ID, $field, true );
$url = false;
                  if ( is_array( $_field ) && isset( $_field[ 'ID' ] )) {
                     $img = $_field[ 'ID' ];
$img = wp_get_attachment_image_src( $img, 'large' );
if ( is_array( $img ) ) {
                        $url = $img[0];
}
}
                  $_field[ 'image_src' ] = $url;
                  $data[ $post->ID ][ $field ] = $_field;
}
}
}
}
}
return $data;
if ( $respond ) {
```

```
        return $this->create_resp( $reqst, $argz, $data );
} else {
return $data;
}
}
```

From the preceding example, you can easily notice that it is a mix of post and meta fields, as well as functions that will have to defined by a parent e-commerce plugin.

Summary

While creating custom routes, we are getting a fantastic RESTful API server that will give us powerful tools for creating our custom APIs, and the fact that WordPress REST API is adding a useful set of default routes to our site is only in our favor.

I would also advise you to make your own default route to make use of any method that you would find suitable or usable.

You have now mastered how to create and add custom routes using REST API in WordPress. Now, our next step will be to power full-fledged applications using WordPress and harness the potential of REST API for that purpose.

6

Creating a Simple Web App using WordPress REST API

So far, we have learnt how to send and receive POST and GET requests in REST API using WordPress, as well as working with posts and post metadata, categories and tags, among other things. As we proceed further with our learning guide, we will now focus on how to create a frontend for our website or app.

Overview

The whole process of content rendering from frontend content to JavaScript or other programming languages that are relatable to frontend is provided by the WordPress REST API, which provides us with the ability to transfer the said process of frontend. JavaScript will then provide us with the opportunity to increase the interactivity and its performance, thus the arisen necessity of making use of it.

This chapter will mainly focus on the process of creating the front-end system for an application or website, all this without disrupting the use of WordPress for managing the content, accomplished by making use of the WordPress REST API. The following chapters will then cover the creation of single page websites, which are powered by the very same WordPress REST API architecture in such a way that its entire frontend capabilities are divided from WordPress.

Setting up your WordPress site

To get started with our site and set it up as the backend for a WordPress-separated kind of frontend we will need to install the WordPress REST API plugin, which would represent the only technical aspect of this whole process.

WordPress, being an ever-growing **Content Management System** (**CMS**) that is moving towards a fully-fledged application framework, brings up the requirement and necessity for new APIs. The REST API Plugin is an easy to use and understand foundation framework that will help you create these APIs, including the core APIs as well.

The plugin provides an accessible and hassle-free way of using the REST APIs, including APIs for the core. The plugin provides an easy to use REST API, which will then be available via HTTP. You will then grab your site's data in some simple JSON format which would include users, posts, taxonomies, and so on. Updating or retrieving data will be as easy as sending an HTTP request. To get site posts using this plugin, you will have to send a GET request, update the user ID and then make use of a PUT request.

The WP API includes an easy-to-use, backbone models-based JavaScript API that allows plugin developers to get up and running without having any need to know the details of how to get connected. It also displays a simple and accessible interface to WP Query, post meta API, the posts API, users API and revisions API, and so on. Chances are that if you can do it with WordPress, then you can do it with WP API.

WP API also includes an easy-to-use JavaScript API based on Backbone models, allowing plugin and theme developers to get up and running without needing to know anything about the details of getting connected. And in case you run into a trouble, you have the documentation at your fingertips, at all times.

We will then proceed to setup our simple application in WordPress with the help of REST API. As you have probably guessed by now, we will be using JSON to interact with our project. We will call it remotely, and focus on AJAX requests to carry data back and forth.

Cross origin problems and bugs

One of the most common issues that developers run into when working with a separate front-end are the restrictions of cross-origins, which place various restraints, and which you can read more about here (`https://developer.mozilla.org/en-US/docs/Web/HTTP/Access_control_CORS`). Most browsers will most likely not let you load content from one site to another if they are served from two separate domains, the reason for this being some very understandable security concerns that might relate to exploitation that can happen during this process. The AJAX requests would then be prevented from succeeding when requesting data form a separate domain, and to avoid an issue of that kind we would have to be sure that all of the **Cross-Origin Resource Sharing** (**CORS**) headers are set in place correctly.

CORS is a spec of the W3C, which allows cross-domain communication straight away from the browser. It builds on top of the HTTP request object and then allows idioms like same-domain requests to happen. It's pretty easy to use CORS, which is manifested by adding a few special response headers that will allow a site to access another's data. CORS allows coordination between the client and the server, and if you're a client-side developer, then you are shielded from this kind of detail.

Theoretical approach aside, it is important to see that CORS headers can be set in a global manner for any WordPress site, which will lead you to set the header to apply only to the REST API's output. All of the headers, which would include CORS headers, have got to be output before any HTML content. Another point is that by default all of the CORS headers are set by the REST API at the `rest_pre_serve_request` filter, which will then change the headers you sent there, and should remove the function of `rest_send_cors_headers` that are hooked by default and will provide the same CORS default headers.

What we will do here is to allow requests to come from any origin by simply setting the appropriate CORS header correctly, which would be accomplished like this:

```
remove_filter('rest_pre_serve_request', 'rest_send_cors_headers');
add_filter('rest_pre_serve_request', function($value)  {

header('Access-Control-Allow-Origin: *');

header('Access-Control-Allow-Methods: POST, GET, OPTIONS, PUT, DELETE');

header('Access-Control-Allow-Credentials: true');
return $value;
});
```

Different situations require different technical approaches, and while we have chosen one of the easiest methods for this one, it is important to admit that it might not be the best way to go in other situations. In the code above, the asterisk will be replaced with a specific URL that will allow access to that site via a remote REST API.

To add more than one CORS header, you will have to detect the referring site before setting the header, as otherwise the access will be fully denied. Applying the preceding exposed method, however, will let you set the header if you want to allow requests to originate from the referring site.

This will be done by defining an array of acceptable domains, which checks the origin domain (like in `$_SERVER['HTTP_ORIGIN'];`) within the array, and if that is it-that's what will be set as the allowed domain. Preview the code below for how to achieve that:

```
remove_filter ('rest_pre_serve_request', 'rest_send_cors_headers');

add_filter ('rest_pre_serve_request', function($value){
$origin = get_http_origin();
if ( $origin && in_array( $origin, array('example_content', 'example2'
) ) ) {
header('Access-Control-Allow-Origin:'.esc_url_raw($origin));
header('Access-Control-Allow-Methods: POST, GET, OPTIONS, PUT, DELETE');
header('Access-Control-Allow-Credentials:true');
}
return $value;
});
```

The preceding example makes use of a safe way to get the value key of `HTTP_ORIGIN` in the global `$_SERVER`, which is the function within WordPress named `get_http_origin()`.

Your next step will be to check whether the originated URL request is contained in the array of allowed domains, and if that is the case, it will check if the domains are used for the CORS header. If it's not there, it means that the CORS header is simply not set.

One thing to be noticed is that there's the probability of security issues if you have a lot of content on your website, as requesting too many posts at once could be used as an exploit within a DDoS attack on your website.

Handling multiple requests

Regarding potential security issues, we have briefly discussed these above; we will now try to look over a few effective security measures. It might be a concern if you have set a CORS header to allow any domain to access the REST API remotely, and even if you haven't, issues might arise because of how origin headers can be faked.

All parameters for making post queries by the REST API will have a filter, which is dynamically creating using the pattern of `rest_query_var-<name-of-filter>`. This supposes that you can override almost any value that is set for the `posts_per_page filter`, which would then be hooked up to `rest_query_var-posts_per_page`.

There is a recommendation to limit the maximum amount you intend on using in your app, and for an example, take a look at the following code where we used 20 posts per page:

```
add_filter('rest_query_var-posts_per_page', function( $posts_in_page) {
if ( 20 < intval( $posts_per_page ) ) {
$posts_in_page = 20;
}
return $posts_in_page;
});
```

This filter will only work if the number of posts per page will exceed `20`, and if it does, the value is changed to the corresponding number, `20`. As a result of this, a request to `wp/v2/posts?filter[post_in_page]=7` will return seven posts, as you might have noticed, and any request greater than our pre-defined value of `20` will still return `20`, not the larger number used as a value.

Now that we have covered most of the learning process, we will focus on some further optimization measures to make sure our websites and apps work faster and well.

Optimization measures

In this part of our tutorial, we will overview some methods that will help us to improve the optimization of our sites. The REST API uses `WP_Query` for posts and `WP_User_Query` for users, and as a result most of the same methods that are used to improve the optimization of our sites will be mentioned here. The REST API doesn't reinvent how posts or any other kind of information will be queried within the database, but instead makes use of the techniques mentioned previously. `WP_Query` will leverage object caching, thus, using any persistent object cache, will improve its performance no matter how it was used.

One of the most common WordPress optimization strategies is page caching. This, however, has no effect here because it will serve static HTML files of users to the frontend of your website. The REST API will come through with a filter that will allow us to intercept requests, and will correspondingly serve a response directly, as the file serving requests are not generating frontend HTML.

By using the WP-TLC-Transients library for cache handling, we will be creating a caching system that will then check if it has already served a request for that URL, and if it has returned a response. If these were not the server, however, REST API will build the response and then cache it before serving the response.

The `json_pre_dispatch` filter makes this possible by exposing two variables, `$result` and `$server`. `$result` is `false` by default, and if it doesn't return a `false` value, it is then used as the response and the rest of the plugin is skipped. The second variable, `$server`, will be the JSON server itself, which will then allow you to provide a proper format for all your results, for example:

```
add_filter (rest_pre_dispatch', 'rest_cache_get', 10, 2);
function rest_cache_get( $result, $server ) {
        //Checking to see if rebuild callback exists, if it does not then
return unmodified.

if ( ! function_exists('rest_cache_rebuild')) {
return $result;
}

//get the REST request and hash it to make the transient key
$request_uri = $_SERVER['REQUEST_URI'];
$key = md5($request_uri);



//return the cache or build cache
$result = transient(__FUNCTION__ .$key)

->updates_with('rest_cache_rebuild', array($server))

->expires_in(600)

->get();
return $result;
}
```

An existent transient called **transient library** was called for the hashed value of the URL that was requested. If it is not found, the function of `rest_cache_rebuild` will be called, which will then generate the cached value and pass the variable of the `$server` to it. The dispatch method is used for this function of the server's class, to set in motion the REST API's default behavior, and to create a response that will be something like this:

```
function rest_cache_rebuild( $server ) {

return $server->dispatch();
}
```

Steps to disable the default routes

The WordPress REST API provides a set of standard routes, but they might not all be required for your app, as the default routes were not all specifically designed for it. The REST API will make it simple to add custom endpoints that will have absolutely no limit on how they will be used. In our next chapter, we will be covering the process of creating custom routes that, for application development, will work better than using the usual default routes method.

- When working with default routes, you should be careful about doing so as that will be counted on several third-party tools.
- There is a possibility that the WordPress admin will start utilizing the REST API, which will remove the default routes and will break the admin.
- The registration of default routes will be removed, which, by getting rid of the hook where the endpoints, in a manner similar to following code:

```
remove_action( 'rest_api_init', 'create_initial_rest_routes', 0 );
```

Another technical aspect is understanding that getting rid of a particular endpoint is not always that easy, and might require somewhat more advanced techniques. To achieve our desired result, we will have to use the filter called `rest_endpoints`, which will then expose all of the registered endpoints before requests are served. If you wanted to remove all endpoints for *fun*, you would need to look for URLs for the endpoints in the `wp/v2` namespace that include *fun* somewhere in the URL, like this:

```
add_filter('rest_endpoints',function($endpnts) {
    foreach($endpnts as $endpoint => $args) {
          if(isset($args['namespace']) && 'wp/v2' == $args['namespace']) {
                $parsed_route = explode('/',$endpoint);
if ( in_array( 'fun', $parsed_route ) ) {
                unset($endpnts[$endpoint]);
}
}
}
return $endpnts;
});
```

No custom routes for `fun` will be affected, as we will only be working with the namespace for the default routes.

More about WP REST API

It has now been well over a decade since Matt Mullenweg brought the blogging content management system to the world that we know so well today. Since the beginning, it has grown well to become the most used CMS, which no longer only covers blogging, but has come to serve all kinds of needs including e-commerce and corporate websites.

REST API has grown to serve as one of the latest features being added to WordPress, which provides more room for interaction and communication between applications and WordPress itself. Because the REST API provides us with the ability to add and then retrieve content from any client without having WordPress installed, it will provide us with an amazing possibility to build custom apps. Overall, we would consider that development inside and in pair with WordPress can now be done without much coding.

Within this set of series, we will be going through the methods for making use of this great API that will provide better user experiences for both developers and end-users, which were probably either impossible, or way harder, to create back in the day.

Within this chapter, we will be making use of some basic resources and concepts that you should already be familiar with, such as the HTTP, JSON and REST itself.

The REST architecture

In order to take a closer look at the REST architecture we shall assess the basics of how it works and is set up, this being one of the first steps in our further encounters that will provide a path for application development and pairing by making use of the REST architectural style.

In its essence, REST is built in a way that helps to distribute the hypermedia application that will further link resources and make it possible for communication to happen by exchanging various representations of its resource state. The resources we are talking about are what the REST architecture is made of, and will be considered to be at the foundation of all websites and scripts overall. In regard to WordPress, the resources are pages, posts, users and comments that interact with provided resources that are in turn used to identify a resource. When a RESTful service is used, it will then make it a first task to address one of the underlying resources, which in its manifestation can have different representations (file format for some file types, and so on). In regard to the connection with URIs, these URIs can only be pointed at a single resource even if one of these resources can have several URIs within it.

The resources that are currently supported by the WP REST API are posts, pages, user databases and media. Such data as post metas and post types would also be considered to be a part of the resources that are supported. HTTP verbs would then be used in order to apply a set of various actions upon the previously mentioned resources.

HTTP verbs

Within the REST API, operations of the C-R-U-D type are allowed by making use of the HTTP, which in turn is used by REST, which will set a limited number of request verbs that will be used to perform an action of creating, updating, deleting, checking or retrieving data exclusively to provided resources and its verbs, if that is the case.

The verbs will be very well described and, as mentioned above, are used to perform a CRUD action in one instance, or to assist a client in determining if a resource exists and what exactly HTTP verbs are, which will provide a clear idea of what actions can be further applied. In this state, a GET request of a kind shall retrieve information, and no matter how many times a client performs calls upon it, the state of a resource might not even get affected.

For us to get all posts using the WP REST API, we will make use of this endpoint, which in turn will return a set of all post entities that are there:

```
GET wp/v2/posts
```

If we would like a particular entity to be returned, and a post with a unique ID, we will apply the following endpoint:

```
GET wp/v2/posts/150
```

Requests such as PUT and POST will replace and create entities with new versions, respectively. If we want to create a new post and send the request body that will be looked at throughout our series, we will apply the following POST request by using WP REST API:

```
POST wp/v2/posts
```

And this PUT request will provide the post with the ID of `100`.

```
PUT wp/v2/posts/150
```

A request such as `delete` will remove a resource from the system, but it will be repeatable with the PUT request, and will have an identical effect upon the system. A RESTful service will provide two more verbs for CRUD actions and those will be the OPTIONS and HEAD verbs, which will come in handy when a client needs to check when a resource is available on the system and what kind of actions will be supported by them, allowing further system explorations and actions to be performed.

Endpoints and routes

Endpoints represent functions, which will then be available through the API and will perform any kind of actions including, but not limited to, creating and retrieving posts and users. The endpoints will rely upon the HTTP verb that is associated with them and will make it retrieve all available posts. The route of the preceding endpoint will be as follows:

```
wp/v2/posts
```

A route will then be assigned one or several endpoints, depending on the HTTP verbs. The route we have just mentioned will need to have an endpoint similar to this if the aim is to create a new posting:

```
POST wp/v2/posts
```

The following route will have a post entity with an ID equal to `100`, which will eventually have three endpoints:

```
wp/v2/posts/150
```

- `GET wp/v2/posts/150`: Will retrieve the post that has the ID of `150`. It will trigger the `get_item()` method.
- `PUT wp/v2/posts/150`: Will update the post that is attributed the ID of `150`. This will trigger the `update_item()` method.
- `DELETE wp/v2/posts/500`: Will delete the post with the ID of `150`. This will trigger the `delete_item()` method.

The HTTP response codes will be a part of our response to the requests by returning any response that contains an HTTP status code of any kind. The codes with numbers will then have predefined definitions linked to them. Another idea to assess is the fact that the response of the server will depend on the HTTP verbs and their types or methods applied to send a request. While working with the WP REST API, a bunch of common HTTP response codes will be encountered, which you should look up if you're not yet familiar with them.

JSON REST API for WordPress

In this posting, we will cover the REST and JSON advantages that should make it clear why we like to use them anyway. The basic theory is that an interlink is required between the client and server, and the weight put upon the server connection is another, so JSON is used to ensure a more lightweight method, unlike known XML methods. As long as JSON uses text to store data, most programming languages will be friendly with it, and will pair easily and seamlessly, working as a global connector in the mechanism of exchanging data between platforms. When we are using APIs like the one that we are talking about now, the content and other data of our WordPress website can be accessed by other clients that are stored externally. Remote clients will then interact with our site to create and update new content, and can retrieve some content from existing WordPress sites and any other ones.

There is unlimited room for constant improvement in how the WP REST API can be used, such as mobile and desktop applications that will pair to your WordPress website, single page applications, advanced server-side integration and so on.

JSON REST APIs in WordPress

Before there were APIs that relied on JSON, they used to interact with the XML-RPC API, which was not as lightweight, easy-to-use, and flexible, which is why APIs have evolved to REST ones. The JSON API has started to become one of the foundations that many plugin developers have taken as their ammo and will be included in the core WordPress in one of its future releases, stipulated to be 4.7. The REST API plugin is currently in continuous development and will be supported as it keeps being improved.

WP REST API at the moment

The WP Rest API has been partially included in the 4.4 version, and will be merged in two different phases: the infrastructure code merge and the endpoints merge. The first phase will consist of the infrastructure code that will become the foundation of WP REST API, which will then include linking and embedding of all the APIs, but will however not include any endpoints or classes. In its second phase, the endpoints will merge and be incorporated in the 4.7 version of WordPress and will map external data in JSON format into native WordPress data types. This will then allow developers to implement custom APIs within their plugins and themes. Not only will this provide advantages for developers, but with the clear evolution of this technology, we will definitely see development and improvement in all other areas that surround the APIs.

Tools

During this tutorial series, we will be making use of HTTP clients that we will use to send a request to the server and preview the received results. We will need a tool that we will use to create quick HTTP requests that will let us view responses from the server and then test configuration and authentication. A tool that will help us with this task is Postman for Google Chrome, although there are other alternatives depending on the browser you're using. The tool we have chosen, Postman, will allow us to create quick HTTP requests that will provide us with different methods for making HTTP requests and will test the configuration for the authentication.

Another tool required for our server is the WP-CLI, which will be used to manage our WordPress installation remotely from within the console without needing to open the browser window, which will be used in the WP-CLI in part with OAuth 1.0a authentication. Some XML demo data will be used to create pages and posts.

Installing the plugin

Our next step will consist of setting up the plugin, which can be found in its official repository. We will be using the REST API plugin that is currently in its 2.0 version, but in a beta state. It is to be noted that developers do not recommend installing this on any server that contains a website used for any other purpose than testing, as the plugin still has several flaws and might be unstable in certain environments. The plugin can be installed on its official page or the GitHub repository that will go to your `/wp-content/plugins` directory. Fire up the terminal and install the plugin like this:

```
$git pull https://github.com/WP-API/WP-API.git
```

After following this procedure, the plugin will go to the `WP-API/directory` and will then be activated from your WordPress administration panel.

After installing the plugin, we are not limited in how we use the API, and can use it on several sites as long as they have the plugin enabled, and to perform a check on other sites we will send a `HEAD` request to the site by using the `HTTP` client, like this:

```
$ HEAD http://myexample.com/
```

A response of the kind will then be received in the response header.

The `LINK` header will further point to the routes located at the root of WP API, which for us will be located at: `http://localserver/wordpress-api/wp-json/`

The API is then going to be discovered by making a query for the respective `<link>` element within DOM, performed like this:

```
(function( $ ) {
    var $link = $( 'link[rel="https://github.com/WP-API/WP-API"]' );
    var api_root = $link.attr( 'href' );
})( jQuery );
```

At this point, we will be ready to retrieve content from the site using the WP REST API when a respective authenticated request is performed.

Going further

Within this part of our tutorial, we have assessed the foundation of WP REST API and how it works. We have gone through the architectural foundation of REST, and the processes that are its foundation. The development state, and how the plugin will evolve, has also been part of our discussion, and will shed some light on the ongoing improvement behind the plugin.

One matter of concern for us in our next section is going to be the methods used for authentication that are supported by the API.

WP REST API – setting up and using basic authentication

So far, we have started with the basics in regard to REST API's architecture and how it will help us pair websites with applications, but now we will move on to creating a protocol that will be used for basic authentication on the server and sending authenticated requests. These requests will be used to perform further tasks in regard to the REST API.

In this section, we will overview the process of sending authenticated requests of various kinds and methods that will be helpful and useful in the next parts of this tutorial.

Authentication

Authentication is defined as the process that helps to identify individuals depending on the unique nature of their credentials. It will ensure that the credentials provided correspond to those stored in the database, and will not be of much help beyond this. In regard to WP REST API, a user will be required to have privileges that will allow him to perform tasks, yet because the identity has to undergo a check, this is where authentication will play its role.

WP REST API authentication

There are currently three methods of authentication when talking about REST API. These three solutions are basic authentication, cookie authentication and OAuth authentication. Every method listed above has its concrete and precise purpose.

The method used by default by WordPress is authentication by cookies, which is how it determines the prerogatives any user has. This provided, we can use this straight away with WP REST API. Using the other two methods will require some plugins to be installed, which are not available within the core of WordPress.

Basic authentication

This kind of authentication is the most common and basic way to authenticate HTPP, in which a user's credentials are sent with the headers of the request from the server, and then the request is received back, along with encoded credentials that are sent in the `Authorization` header field as following:

```
Authorization: Basic {base64_encode(username:password)}
```

If the username is `whatever` and the password is set as `1111` a header field like this would be sent with the request:

```
Authorization: Basic dHV0c3BsdXM6MTIzNDU2
```

However, this method is not used by open networks given its insecurities in terms of how easy it would be to decode it.

Installing the plugin

The plugin is available on the official GitHub repository, so all we have to do to install it is just clone it in our plugins directory and simply activate it. Turn the `sudo` rights on in order to run the command and clone our plugin at `/wp-content/plugins`:

```
$ sudo git clone https://github.com/WP-API/Basic-Auth.git
```

The terminal will then require your password, after which it will continue with the process of cloning within the directory. Upon cloning, activate the plugin within your administration panel.

Postman requests

In this section we will take a look at the process of sending authenticated requests by making use of the tool I spoke of in a previous section—**Postman**. It will allow us to send a request only using the basic authentication method we already briefly covered. In order to fulfill an authenticated request you will have to go to the **Authentication** tab, from where you have to use the basic authentication method, which will ask for credentials, yielding an encoded version of those same credentials. A request can then be sent as a test, in our case we would be deleting a post, like this:

```
DELETE http://something/wp-json/wp/v2/posts/25
```

If everything is performed successfully, a status code with the **200 OK** ID will indicate the post has been deleted.

Authenticated requests from the command line

If you are not fond of using the available browser tools, the command line can be used to send the same requests, which would use the `curl` equivalent of a preceding request:

```
"curl --request DELETE -I --user  admin:password
http://something/wp-json/wp/v2/posts/25"
```

The server will then respond with a success message that will indicate the action was completed successfully and flawlessly. The `request` option will then specify the request method that is going to be used, which in our case will be `DELETE`. The `-x` alternative is also admitted for the `--request` option.

JavaScript authenticated requests

In case you are using any client-side JavaScript framework, authorization headers can be sent for the desired interaction with WP API. The `DELETE` request would then be sent by another `jQuery.ajax()` method like this:

```
$.ajax({
    url: 'http://something/wp-json/wp/v2/posts/25',
    method: 'DELETE',
    crossDomain: true,
    beforeSend: function ( xrh ) {
        xrh.setRequestHeader( 'Authorization', 'Basic ' +
Base64.encode( 'username:password' ) );
    },
    success: function( data, txtStatus, xrh ) {
        console.log( data );
        console.log( xrh.status );
    }
});
```

In this example, the `BASE64` is considered to be an object used for encoding a string.

This is a way of cross-browser encoding of a string within JavaScript.

The `Authorization` header was used in the preceding example, and the `setRequestHeader()` method within `xhr` object was passed as an argument to the `beforeSend()` method.

Another thing to assess is whether headers with `Access-Control-Allow-Headers` will always allow a field like `Authorization` on the server and can then be enabled by adding a line of code within your WordPress `.htaccess` file:

```
Header always set Access-Control-Allow-Headers Authorization Header always
set
```

The response displayed will then be echoed within your browser's console.

WP HTTP API for authenticated requests

If your aim is to interact remotely with any other WordPress site that is on our installation, the best method for sending HTTP requests is thought to be the `WP HTTP API`. It is also considered that the code provided will send a `DELETE` request to any other WordPress installation that has the basic authentication turned on within `WP REST API`.

It's good that we have gone through how basic authentication works, as this will come in very handy in further parts of the tutorial, in which we will mainly be using this method for performing any kind of data manipulation.

Status check

Within this part of the tutorial, we have exclusively focused on the basic authentication method supported by the `WP REST API`. As stipulated here, using this method on live websites is dangerous and foolish, given how easily credentials can be decoded and then further abused.

Another thing we have looked at in this article is the process of testing the authentication method we discussed in detail, making us ready to move on to a more complicated method of authentication named **OAuth**. We will be covering this in specific detail as we move on.

WP REST API – setting up and using advanced authentication

Our previous section covered the basics of the WP REST API and the HTTP authentication that were on the server, which let us install the plugin available on GitHub, courtesy of the development team behind WP REST API. So far, we have only overviewed a method of authentication that will let us use it in a testing environment, but the time has come for us to look into more serious, advanced means of authentication that will be secure enough for us to use on an actual server, and will not compromise the credentials exposed to the requests.

In this part of our tutorial, we will go through the process of setting up the OAuth authentication method that will be used with the WP REST API plugin. We will install the OAuth server plugin and then generate an access token that will help us with the pairing of a conventional application, all this combined with a theoretical overview of the method itself and how it functions.

OAuth authentication

The OAuth authentication method is an open method of securing client application and the access that it has to the resources located on the server. The authorization will then obtain partial access to an HTTP service that is going to allow further access to an application to obtain access on its behalf. With OAuth, the user will be able to have access to private data from one server to another server's resource without needing to share their identities.

Besides users, mobile and desktop applications will also gain access to the resources on the server, and the permissions that will be granted will be either of a limited kind or fully permissive, which we will take a look at soon.

OAuth security concerns

The second version of OAuth will not support any encryption, client verification or signature and there have been reports of major security flaws that have been addressed. The biggest concern about OAuth's security failure is the vulnerability to phishing and that there have been stolen emulations of credentials, which even two-factor authentication cannot prevent. We are only mentioning this as we are looking to bring up any concerns that have been heard, and leave you to take the decision that you consider to be correct.

OAuth 2.0

The second generation of OAuth is the newest protocol, which is not backward compatible with OAuth 1.0. The second version will put a distinct focus upon simplicity in the process of providing authorization for web, desktop, and mobile applications. It is currently used by Facebook, Google and major other services, which recommend this authentication mechanism for use with their APIs.

OAuth authentication flow

OAuth authorization makes use of token credentials, which are provided by the server when an appropriate request is issued and authenticated. These tokens, which are linked to the server, are then used by an application to receive access to protected resources (credentials). These authorization tokens then have a particularly limited period in which they are active, and are revoked by the server upon any request asking for this.

The process of OAuth authorization is broken down into several steps, which are:

Oauth_callback function

The client sends a request to obtain one of the tokens, which are considered to be a temporary credential at the endpoint URI. The server will then verify whether the received request is legit, and if that seems to be the case, a request token will be provided as a result. It moves forward with the client pointing the user towards the server for further request authorization, which is concluded by adding an `oauth_token` that was obtained in the previous step. A further authorization at server level takes place upon the provision of the required credentials, which yields one of two things. In the case of an `oauth_callback` URI provision, the server will redirect the client towards that specific URI, or if the `oauth_callback` is not provided, the server would simply display a value of the `oauth_verifier` that will let the resource handler manage client requests manually.

OAuth_verifier function

Upon receiving the `oauth_verifier` token, the client asks the server for token credentials by sending another request to the token request endpoint URI. The server verifies whether the request is valid and will grant any of the token credentials: `oauth_token_secret`. And as a finale, the client makes use of the provided token credentials, which will be used to access the protected resources on the server.

This more complex process is necessary when considering developing clients that would connect with the API. The main task of a client would be to make the process easier for the end-user, but given the fact that we will make the most of the WP REST API, we will start with only the strictly necessary steps.

Endpoint URIs are exposed within the server response when checking for the API, and thus the authentication with OAuth for WP REST API makes use of exposing URIs provided by the server.

OAuth installation

Installing the OAuth authentication API within WordPress can sometimes be a tough task. OAuth enables a temporary credential request endpoint that, using the `wp_scope` parameter, will grant access to the client. The plugin, which is available on the official GitHub repository will only support version 4.4 and above of WordPress.

We will now move forward with cloning the plugin by navigating to the plugins directory within `/wp-content/plugins/`:

```
$ git clone https://github.com/WP-API/OAuth1.git
```

Upon completing the download, we will activate the plugin by making use of the WP CLI:

```
$ wp plugin activate OAuth1
```

That is what we must do in order to set up `OAuth` as a workable authorization method.

Assessing the availability of the OAuth API

Our first check is to see whether the API is enabled on the server or not, and for this we will be making use of a simple GET request that will be sent to the `/wp-json/` endpoint, which will then analyze the status of the response that has been received. A next step is to launch an HTTP client and send another request to the `/wp-json/` endpoint, which would be something like this:

```
GET http://example-site/wp-json/
```

and will return a JSON response.

We have our focus upon on the `oauth1` value that further sends us the `authentication` property value, and has within its properties the following: request, access, version and authorize.

Server responses will usually contain an empty `authorization` property if the OAuth API is not enabled for the site, and the `oauth1` defined object within the `authentication` property will show that the OAuth API has successfully passed.

Application management

When we are done installing the OAuth plugin, we have to register an application, which is possible within the admin dashboard of WordPress, that will then provide us with corresponding generated OAuth credentials to use. The plugin will make use of the functionality provided to create a consumer within the console through the WP CLI plugin, which can be done in the terminal as well, like this:

```
wp oauth1 add --name=<c_name> --description=<c_description>
```

After doing this, the consumer will appear within the registered applications page in the plugin's dashboard, where it can be managed for further modification.

Generating OAuth credentials

Now that our application has been registered, we will move on to begin the OAuth authorization process within the upcoming sections. The typical process of generating OAuth credentials is to acquire temporary credentials, authorize the user, and then finish by exchanging tokens. To implement this whole process we will continue with the tool we started with at the beginning of this tutorial-Postman.

In order to acquire temporary credentials we will be sending a POST request to the `/oauth1/request` endpoint that will be auto-discovered when the server replaces this route with its own one. The POST request we mentioned earlier should cover the `oath_consumer_key` and the `oath_consumer_secret` parameters that will include the last parameter of `oauth_callback`, which should actually match the details of the callback URL that was used when the application was registered.

When making use of the Postman, the `oauth_signature` will be generated automatically and we only have to mention the `oauth_signature_method` parameters.

Make copies of the consumer secret and consumer key parameters, because they will be needed further on, and now, by launching Postman, send a POST request to the temporary credentials request endpoint. The Postman should send another POST request to the temporary token credentials endpoint and then fill in the fields of **consumer key** and **consumer secret** with the data that has just been copied in the preceding step. Updating the request will finish the process and return a success code in the form of a dummy text string.

User authorization

For the user authorization step, we will have to pass the `oauth_token` and `oauth_token_secret` tokens as query parameters:
`http://example-com/oauth1/authorize?oauth_token=<token_here>&oauth_token_secret=<secret_here>`.

You will have to authorize the application, and once that is done, the application will appear within your list of authorized apps within your plugin.

Token exchange

The final step for OAuth authorization is exchanging tokens that were granted only temporary access to ones that have a *longer* lifespan and are considered to be *permanent*. We will start the process in which the exchange happens, the Postman will be launched and configured so that POST requests are sent to the endpoint of the request token. After making use of the OAuth 1.0 option, within the **Authorization** tab we will fill in with consumer-provided data the fields for consumer keys and tokens that will be making use of the `oauth_token` and `oauth_token_secret` parameters respectively.

The parameter of `oauth_verifier` has got to be appended to the URL: `http://example-com/oauth1/access?oauth_verifier=<oauth_verifier_value>`.

Given everything in the process was fine, temporary tokens are no longer of use, given the fact that they have been replaced with *permanent* ones.

Status check

In this part of the tutorial we have taken an in-depth overview of the OAuth authentication solution and how it will interact with third-party applications. Not only have we looked at the theoretical side of this authentication method, and the objective way that it works, we have also taken a closer look at how to actually apply this method in practice.

WP REST API – retrieving data

After going through all the basics related to WP REST API, and assessing how it will actually make it easier for us to develop applications for background pairing with WordPress' backend, we also have to overview the authentication methodology that there is and that should already be set and running to have the WP REST API plugin installed. We have also taken an in-depth look at two methods for server-side authentication, a more simple yet very insecure method of basic authentication, and a more complicated method which is, however, secure enough to be used in real-world environments-namely OAuth.

During this part of the tutorial, we shall start generating authenticated requests, given our progress so far. For testing purposes, we shall stick to basic authentication for the course of this tutorial, but remember one more time that this method of authentication must never be used in real-world examples and has got to be used only in scenarios like this one.

We shall get started by analyzing the structure of a GET request and then move forward by sending data retrieval request to the server, operating with `OPTIONS` requests and then analyzing the received response on the server side.

The GET request

Starting off with the syntax we will be working with, we shall analyze a couple of syntax requests that will be sent to the server, as it will explain the behavioral side of the servers and its future encounters with the WP REST API plugin.

Analyzing this request:

```
$ GET http://localhost/wp-json/wp/v2/posts
```

In this request, we will be sending a GET request to the server, a request that is used to retrieve data from the server it is being sent to. The response we will receive will be in the form of JSON data and will consist of all the post objects.

Regarding its technical structure, the request could be divided into several parts, namely the URL, endpoint prefix, namespace, version and resource. These prefixes and paths would all indicate the location of the server, endpoint prefixes, and the namespace used, including the version of the plugin that has been used along with the desired resource we would like to receive from the server.

The version and namespace are new things in version 2.0 of the plugin, having not been available in previous releases of the plugin, in which the very same request shown previously would take a form similar to this:

```
$ GET http://localhost/wp-json/posts
```

In case we are not looking to retrieve all posts that we called with the request above, and are only interested in receiving a single post, we would have to mention the ID of the resource that we would like to retrieve. In the case presented below, the post with the ID of `100` will be looked for and then retrieved:

```
$ GET /wp/v2/posts/100
```

Besides this, there's also the possibility to search for more specific data as well, like a filtered post with some specific criteria for which we are going to use a `filter[]` syntax. This request will retrieve all posts that have their corresponding category set with an ID of `1`, and could especially be of great help when querying different data at the same time (like categories along posts) especially when there's a link between the two. Anyway, the request would be similar to this:

```
$ GET /wp/v2/posts?filter[cat]=1
```

When working with arguments that take arrays as inputs within the `filter[]` syntax, it is to be assessed.

```
$ GET /wp/v2/posts?filter[category__and][]=1&filter[category__and][]=2
```

Posts that are assigned both the ID of `1` and `2` will be retrieved by the `GET` request. We will get into more details as to how the syntax of filtering works, but for now we shall take a look at the `OPTIONS` request that will make it easy to navigate through the API and at the same time makes it a more proficient way of documenting the HTTP methods. In the next part of our tutorial we will look into the `OPTIONS` requests, and how to handle those.

Options request

The `OPTIONS` request includes all endpoints that correspond to a particular route and provides a list of parameters; these endpoints will provide support for particular CRUD operations.

By using the route of `/wp/v2/posts` and sending a corresponding `OPTIONS` request to it, we will check whether it supports parameters that can then be passed along the GET request to query data, for which you would use any of the tools that allow request sending. We have mentioned Postman for Chrome in our previous series, and you could stick with that. Anyway, back to our request:

```
$ curl -X OPTIONS wp/v2/posts
```

We will now perform another request that will return data in the JSON format and five of its properties, which are endpoints; `methods`; `namespaces`; `schema`, and `_links`.

```
{
    "namespace": "wp/v2",
}
```

As we move on with our tutorial, the namespace property will identify the namespace of our current plugin, which in our case is determined to be `wp/v2`, the `v2` within it clearly representing the version of our plugin, which is 2.0.

```
{
    ...
    "methods": [
        "GET",
        "POST"
    ],
    ...
}
```

The main property here is named `methods`, and it contains an array that will contain all methods supported by the current route, which obviously supports the `POST` and `GET` methods, giving the possibility of using the route `/wp/v2/posts` to manipulate posts.

```
{
    ...
    "endpoints": [
        {
            "methods": [
                "GET"
            ],
            "args": {...}
        },
        {
            "methods": [
                "POST"
            ],
            "args": {...}
        }
    ],
    ...
}
```

The property of `endpoints` displayed in the preceding example contains another array of the supported endpoints for the current route and lists all endpoints of the supported methods. The property will then contain object values that will turn into the properties of `args` and `methods`, which are properties, meant to contain all of the supported arguments, contain the arrays of HTTP methods and provide supported arguments for such methods respectively.

The `GET` method supports arguments that are covered under two main properties, which are `default` and `required`. It is understandable from the functionality point of view, as the attributes would either provide or neglect some prerogatives to arguments (such as showing whether an argument is required or is the default value), depending on the property that it has been provided with.

```
"methods": [
        "GET"
    ],
"args": {
    "context": {
        "required": false,
        "default": "view"
    },
    "page": {
        "required": false,
        "default": 1
    },
    "per_page": {
        "required": false,
        "default": 10
    },
    "filter": {
        "required": false
    }
}
```

By making use of a `GET` request to the index route `/wp-json` we could easily check the availability of an API, which would then list the routes present including the endpoints along their supported arguments and methods. Making use of this will no longer make it necessary to have the routes documented externally.

Retrieving posts from the server

We will move forward with post retrieving from the server by making good use of all the knowledge and techniques we have overviewed over the course of this chapter. In this part, we will be using the REST API to query posts via various filters. This is where we will use the filtering syntax to retrieve posts via its top-level parameter, which is slightly different to retrieving an individual post as we have done earlier.

There are a bunch of common query variables that point by using the GET endpoint. By making use of the context parameter we could easily fetch posts from the server, but as there are more parameters, we won't run into much trouble. For example, the edit parameter will be used for editing, and the view one will be used to list a series of posts. While we could go into detail with an explanation of each parameter, the self-explanatory nature of each will not represent a difficulty in working with them.

The filter[] syntax

One thing to assess about the filter[] syntax is the fact that it will work in pair with the WP_Query() class of WordPress. The pairing, to be precise, does not happen on a connection level, but it's more of an analogy of how we will use the filtering syntax, implying that the querying of posts is concluded in a similar way to when it is done with the WP_Query class.

A request that retrieves a specific number of posts per page makes use of the posts_per_page variable, and that means that the parameters for pagination that are set in place are among the most important ones, provided they help us by displaying a precise amount of posts.

```
$ GET /wp/v2/posts?filter[posts_per_page]=5&filter[paged]=2
```

Take a look at the request above. It involves both the posts_per_page parameter that we have mentioned, and the paged one, which is used in a pair with the first one in order to help us navigate to a specific amount of pages.

Another important use of the filter[] syntax is to actually provide more detailed querying, thus it is possible to add an extra parameter to the syntax that will narrow down the desired fetching by any time unit (such as year, hour, minute and so on).

```
$ GET /wp/v2/posts?filter[year]=2016&filter[monthnum]=06&filter[day]=06
```

The preceding request will narrow our search of published posts to any date we set within the time parameter of the request, in our case 2016-06-06.

It will also be possible to retrieve posts that correspond to various corresponding, and we will trigger the ones we want by using unique IDs or even retrieve posts that exclude posts within one category (also triggered by the category's unique ID). Overall it is to be considered that the filter syntax, as it is supposed to, provides us with the possibility of deep filtering for various details, and thus is another point for flexibility provided by the WP REST API.

Post revisions, categories, tags, and meta

By using querying endpoints of `/posts/<id>/revisions` we will be able to trigger the endpoint to view and restore any edits that have been applied to a post. If we were to retrieve all revisions of a post (having a conventional ID of `10`), we would send this request, which is going to return an array with the revision objects in itself:

```
$ GET /wp/v2/posts/10/revisions
```

As we have seen with the filtering syntax, it is mainly narrowed down to the unique ID of the post or category, thus if we were to retrieve a post that has its revision ID set as `2`, and the ID of the post itself is set at `10`, we would be sending the following request that is going to return a single revision object:

```
$ GET /wp/v2/posts/10/revisions/2
```

By using the preceding example, in a similar way, we could retrieve categories tags and metadata. We are going to perform a search that will retrieve post meta with an ID of `10`, for example purposes:

```
$ GET /wp/v2/posts/10/meta
```

Other resources

At this point, it should be pretty clear how the WP REST API works in retrieving data. The basics we have looked at in the course of this tutorial will help us with our upcoming practical examples, and will of course help you to have a better understanding of how the system works. Overall, it is clear by now that most of the time we will be making use of the `OPTIONS` and `GET` requests in order to retrieve a particular resource or to index endpoints respectively, the process for which should be clear to you by now. One more thing to mention is that over this course we will not be able to provide examples for each and every possibility for the cases we are working with, but the thorough documentation the developers have put in place will definitely help you to not get lost; after all the course itself is pretty explanatory to help you get sorted if you are somehow stuck.

Status check

Our tutorial has laid the foundations for you, providing a clear and understandable path towards creating more unique applications as a final task. The diversity and flexibility WP REST API provides will help in interacting with the entire WordPress ecosystem as a whole and not limit you to small, trivial tasks. As we move forward, we will be looking at how to update, create and delete resources, which should entirely conclude the process.

WP REST API: creating and editing posts

In the previous parts of our tutorial we have gone through the foundations of WP REST API, different authentication methods and of course the process for us to retrieve content from a server, including the retrieval of different resources like posts and categories, which in turn could be narrowed down to even more specific details. We got familiar with the `GET` and `OPTIONS` request that will provide even more insight into how the API works, which should provide you with enough knowledge to be prepared for the more detailed steps that we will be going through in this part.

Our next step is to learn how to work with resources and especially how to create, delete and update them, and then analyze the yielded responses that would be provided by the server.

CRUD methods in routes

CRUD methods are the actions of creating, reading, updating and deleting. As reading has already been covered, we will be moving forward to the remaining three. One thing to realize is that not all routes will support the update and create methods, and in order to check which ones do, we will be sending separate requests to individual routes by using either the `OPTIONS` request, which will be sent to individual routes, or sending a `GET` request to the index route of the `/wp-json`. If we were to do the latter, we would receive an object that contains all routes and their endpoints within the `routes` property.

So, if we wanted to check if the resource supports the `POST`, `PUT`, and `DELETE` method, we would have to start by analyzing the Posts resource, which would display data in these two routes:

```
/wp/v2/posts
/wp/v2/posts/(?P<id>[\d]+)
```

The first route is going to direct us to the existing collection of posts; the `method` property will show that the `/posts` route will support various methods, and a prolonged version of the route like this /posts/(?P<id>[\d]+) will support five different methods, which should be pretty clear:

```
"methods": [
    "GET",
    "POST",
    "PUT",
    "PATCH",
    "DELETE"
],
```

The `/posts` route is helpful if we are looking to either make or create content, but it isn't helpful if we are looking into deeper editing, such as deletion or updating a resource, for which we would have to make use of the /posts/(?P<id>[\d]+) route. One thing to clear up is that a single entity can not be used to generate content, as it simply does not support this action, yet they will help us to update the content. If we were to check which routes will support the `POST`, `GET`, and `DELETE` methods, then we would send an `OPTIONS` request.

Creating and updating posts

As we have stated previously, during the course of this tutorial we will only make use of the basic authentication method, which is only a good solution for testing purposes and not real-life usage. Right now we will check whether our user that we are going to perform some actions on has the `edit_posts` rights attributed to him, and will then send a `POST` request to the route of `/posts`.

If we send a request that is empty in its body, then the server would return a `Bad Request` error given that our request is empty and there's no argument in the body of it that would trigger an actual request and not the error. We would have to send an actual argument along the request if we wanted to receive anything, and there are three main ways of sending these arguments: as an URL parameter; by making use of forms; or our preferred method, which is by sending a JSON object. You can choose your preferred method within your HTTP client, but we will stick to the JSON one for the time being. Sending the request, by performing a very intuitive process of clicking the **Send** button, should yield a post whose status would be set as `draft`. After that we would have the returned post, it would have an `id` attributed so we will be using that in our request to the endpoint:

```
$ POST /wp/v2/posts/21
```

Now we will set our request body to make updates to the "content" and "status" property that will be similar to this:

```
{
    "status": "publish",
    "content": "This is the sample content of the post"
}
```

In order to create a post, which was done by the preceding request, there are three main arguments that will help us do so. The title argument will obviously set the title for the post. The status argument, being self-explanatory, will set the article to be published or drafted, whereas the content argument will require the content of the article to go there. As these arguments are very clear and easy to understand, we will not go in deeper detail. If we wanted to retrieve the supported arguments for creating a post, then we would use a normal OPTIONS request that would be manifested like this:

```
$ OPTIONS /wp/v2/posts
```

Creating and updating post meta

The first thing to do is to use the companion plugin that is provided by the WP RESTAPI developers and is available over at GitHub for you to install (https://github.com/WP-API/wp-api-meta-endpoints).

In order to create a post meta, we would send a POST request to a route like so:

```
/wp/v2/posts/(?P<parent_id>[\d]+)/meta
```

In this, the ID of the parent post will be the unique ID of the post that was created earlier. If we would like to create a post object, we would send another request, which in turn would have a JSON object made of two properties (key; value) which can then be sent to create a post meta.

```
{
    "key": "name",
    "value": "RockingName"
}
```

If you were to send this request to the server, it would return you a successful status code, indicating that the post meta has been created successfully, yet this would only work as long as you were to stick to the string format, which is the only supported format for now.

Creating and updating data

Under this section of the tutorial, we will try to focus on using other forms that would help us create and update resources, and they will be classified as follows:

Sending data as URL parameters

We are now sending a `POST` request for creating a post like this:

```
$ POST /wp/v2/posts?title=the+title&content=this+is+the+content
```

We have chosen this method because the easiest way of sending data along the request, would be to send it as URL parameters. The above request features two parameters: title and content, which are responsible for the appropriate sections within a post. We could then make use of the post ID we have and use a `POST` request like this to have our post meta created:

```
$ POST /wp/v2/posts/XXX/meta?key=name&value=MyName
```

Overall, this method comes in handy when the parameters are not very lengthy, so stick to it when it is the case.

Sending data as a JSON object

By making use of this method, we will be taking the value pair within a JSON object, which should help us pass them to the request. By using HTML and jQuery, we will try to replicate the results we have been achieving by using an HTTP client so far.

```
<form name="post-form" id="post-form">
    <label for="title">Title</label>
    <input type="text" name="title" id="title">
    <label for="status">Status</label>
    <select name="status" id="status">
        <option value="publish">Publish</option>
        <option value="draft">Draft</option>
    </select>
    <label for="content">Content</label>
    <textarea name="content" id="content"></textarea>
    <input type="submit" name="submit" value="Submit">
</form>
```

The preceding code will be made up of three main fields, for content, status and title. We will then submit the form and will receive a piece of JavaScript code like this:

```
var postForm = $( '#post-form' );
var jsonData = function( form ) {
    var arrData = form.serializeArray(),
        objData = {};
    $.each( arrData, function( index, element ) {
        objData[element.name] = element.value;
    });
    return JSON.stringify( objData );
};
postForm.on( 'submit', function( e ) {
    e.preventDefault();
    $.ajax({
        url: 'http://example/wp-json/wp/v2/posts',
        method: 'POST',
        data: jsonData( postForm ),
        crossDomain: true,
        contentType: 'application/json',
        beforeSend: function ( xhr ) {
            xhr.setRequestHeader( 'Authorization',                    'Basic
username:password' );
        },
        success: function( data ) {
            console.log( data );
        },
        error: function( error ) {
            console.log( error );
        }
    });
});
```

The `/wp/v2/posts` route will be the one to receive the AJAX request that has been sent upon submission of the previous code piece. Upon submission, the HTML form will be converted to a JSON format, which is then used by the `$.ajax()` method and its `data` property. By using the `contentType` property we will be setting the content type to `application/json`. When the request is sent to the `/wp/v2/posts` route, a new post is created, yet not before we include an `Authorization` header that is used by the basic authentication method that we previously overviewed. This is the method of making use of the JSON format to send data along the request where the source of this JSON object can be practically anything except an HTML form. There might be the need to set the `Access-Control-Allow-Headers` header field to have the `Content-Type` and `Authorization` values, which can be done in the `.htaccess` file within WordPress.

Sending data using forms

Another method of sending data along the request is to make use of HTML forms that must contain fields with the attribute of `name`, which will be an argument name whose value of fields will serve as the value of these arguments.

```
var postForm = $( '#post-form' );
postForm.on( 'submit', function( f ) {
    e.preventDefault();
    $.ajax({
        url: 'http://example/wp-json/wp/v2/posts',
        method: 'POST',
        data: postForm.serialize(),
        crossDomain: true,
        beforeSend: function ( xrh ) {
            xhr.setRequestHeader( 'Authorization', 'Basic
username:password' );
        },
        success: function( data ) {
            console.log( data );
        }
    });
});
```

Here we have used the very same HTML form that we used in the previous instance, including an extra piece that will help us create a new post. The key difference between the preceding code and the one in a previous example is that the `jsonData()` method has been removed and we are now sending the form data in some kind of string format by making use of the `serialize()` method that is provided by jQuery. As a last step, we would have to send form data within our HTTP Client, and for this you have to use an option of `format-data`, which in the case of Postman is located under the **Body** tab. As a last mention, the arguments will be defined in key pairs that are then going to be used to send along the desired request.

Uploading media via multipart/form-data

The `multipart/form-data` content type will be used when dealing with binary data if there's a need to upload images or other files to the server. Because the very same encoding type makes use of binary data, it will be used to upload various file types to the server. The following example will make use of a piece of jQuery code that will be responsible for the functionality to upload images to the server and the `input[type="file"]`, which will be the foundation of our HTML.

The following HTML form would be:

```
<form name="image-form" id="image-form">
    <label for="image-input">File</label>
    <input name="image-input" id="image-input" type="file">
    <input type="submit" value="Upload">
</form>
```

And upon the submission of the form, the following JavaScript would be executed:

```
var imageForm = $( '#image-form' ),
    fileInput = $('#file'),
    formData = new FormData();
imageForm.on( 'submit', function( m ) {
    e.preventDefault();
    formData.append( 'file', fileInput[0].files[0] );
    $.ajax({
        url: 'http://example/wp-json/wp/v2/media',
        method: 'POST',
        data: formData,
        crossDomain: true,
        contentType: false,
        processData: false,
        beforeSend: function ( xrh ) {
            xhr.setRequestHeader( 'Authorization', 'Basic
username:password' );
        },
        success: function( data ) {
            console.log( data );
        },
        error: function( error ) {
            console.log( error );
        }
    });
});
```

In this example, the `FormData` object is initialized, leading to providing interfaces in a way that would construct a set of form fields that would use the exact same format as the `multipart/form-data` encoding type, which upon submission will be prevented by the `.preventDefault()` method.

The data that is going to be passed in the `data` property of the `jQuery.ajax()` method will be processed into a query string. We are giving a property of `false` to both `ContentType` and `processData` with the purpose of preventing the passage of data into the `data` property of jQuery and also preventing `application/x-www-form-urlencoded` from reaching the server as a default content type. As discussed previously, an authentication of a user with `edit_posts` privilege is required, thus we would set the `Authorization` header.

Deleting data

As with deleting data, the WP REST API is a very simple system that is going to send a `DELETE` request, which will be triggered towards a particular resource. In order to delete a post with a unique ID, we will send a `DELETE` request as follows:

```
$ DELETE /wp/v2/posts/100?force=true
```

This request will permanently delete the post and not trash it., The `force` argument is responsible for the permanent response, meaning that removing it from the preceding request would result in the post being sent to trash, and not facing permanent deletion. This is worth mentioning because the reasons behind performing deletions are unknown, so everyone can easily decide for themselves whether they want the post to be permanently gone or not.

Status check

This part of the tutorial has been dedicated to CRUD operations for various kinds of resources by making good use of the WP REST API, and the various methods used as alternatives that we have gone through in this section will come in handy. As we are approaching the end of our tutorial, it is worth mentioning that in the last part of our tutorial we will focus on the internal structure of the WP REST API and its classes, as well as working with the API with the purpose of manipulating responses received from the server.

WP REST API: internals and customization

In this last part of our tutorial series on WP REST API, we will be looking at how the internals of the WP REST API work and modifying server responses for our default endpoints to contain custom fields.

Internal classes and methods of WP REST API

WP REST API has two main categories of classes, and those are endpoint and infrastructure classes. The endpoint classes cover the CRUD actions over resources like posts and comments that we overviewed in the last chapter. The infrastructure classes are covering classes that lie at the foundation of the API. In the following example, we will be looking at each of those two classes in detail.

The endpoint classes within the WP REST API are responsible for performing actions of creating, reading, updating and deleting, which include different controllers like the `WP_REST_Posts_Controller` and various others that are united within a more general class named `WP_REST_Controller`.

This patterned class that provides the means for modifying data has different methods included in itself, which end with `_item()` suffix but start with a CRUD-related operation, so a typical method would be `create_item()` amongst others. These classes can be thoroughly researched and understood if you address the available documentation.

Infrastructure classes

When bringing up infrastructure classes, we should mention that there are three main ones in place, namely the `WP_REST_SERVER`; `WP_REST_REQUEST`, and `WP_REST_RESPONSE` classes, which we will be looking at in a second.

WP_REST_Server

The `WP_REST_Server` core class is meant to server requests, register routes and prepare appropriate responses that would then be passed over to the client in case an error pops up, wrapping up the message body and the error code of the error, which in the last instance would check whether the `Authorization` method was in place or not. The endpoint we have been working with during this tutorial is `/wp-on`, and it is to be stated that it checks for all the capabilities and admitted routes regarding a website. When it comes to serving requests and responses, it makes use of `WP_Rest_Response` and `WP_REST_Request` accordingly.

WP_REST_Request

The `WP_REST_Request` class is referred to the object of WP REST API, which would contain data from the request of headers and body, which is then passed over by the `WP_REST_Server` class in order to perform the callback function and check if the set parameters are passing along the request, and if not, it sanitizes the data where necessary.

WP_REST_Response

The `WP_Rest_Response` class, as is suggested by the name, contains favorable and necessary data such as the response body and the status code of the response.

Modifying server responses

As we become more familiar with the internal classes and methods that the API has been built upon, we will be analyzing the methods and classes that are the foundation of the API and provide us with the flexible system that is the API we are using today. From a technical standpoint, the WP REST API provides a way of changing the data that is returned by the server for every default route that not every data (such as pages, posts, users, and so on) can always accommodate. The way that the WP REST API functions is pretty straightforward and clear, which is why when you are planning to make changes that would most likely not be expected, developers encourage you to think twice. Among changes that would not be very appropriate are changes of field from a response, or ever deleting a default field. All this can lead to compatibility issues for clients, who expect standard behavior. Adding fields to the returned responses from the server for multiple or single objects is encouraged.

The register_rest_field()

The `register_rest_field()` method relates to adding or updating fields within the response that is returned by the server and will further accommodate three main arguments, `$object_type`; `$attribute`, and `$args`.

The `$object` type will not be a string or array that contains the names of all of the objects that we intend to add the field for, but it will be a good fit if we are looking forward to adding a custom field to a custom post type. The `$atribute` argument appears in the form of a key when the server sends its response, while the `$array` is responsible for holding the other three keys, which are `$get_callback`; `$update_callback`, and `$schema`. They are set in place to be used when it is necessary to receive an update to a value of a custom field, but that does not cover the `$schema` key, which covers the method and variable used to provide a definition for the custom field. While the keys are not mandatory, the capability will not be added in their absence.

Then there is also the `register_rest_field()` method, which will work so that the `$wp_rest_additional_fields` variable will be modified. The array will then hold registered fields by object type and will be returned via a form of response by the server itself. The variable of `$wp_rest_additional_fields` will get added whenever a new field is registered by the previously-mentioned method.

Summary

We have now come to the end of this chapter. Here, you learned how to prepare WordPress to power a simple web app using REST API, as well as how to optimize your app using page caching, and finally, how to modify end points just in case you wish to create something custom.

As we have assessed several times during this chapter, not every specific technique applies to each and every website. However, this does not imply that these methods cannot serve you as general technical guidelines if not practical, technical advice. This chapter also covered the use of the REST API to power another site or application or going through the process of integrating with one or more sites or platforms.

In the next chapter, we will dig deeper and learn further details about the functioning of REST API and its future as well as present usage. However, for now, you are good to go and you can work with REST API in WordPress with your current knowledge. The remaining two chapters will give you added information that you can make use of if you wish to take REST API beyond WordPress.

7
Mastering REST API for Your Projects

We have now covered all the coding bits and the details of REST API for WordPress. At this stage, you are equipped to create simple apps using WordPress REST API, as well as to work with GET and POST requests, perform AJAX queries, and do a lot more.

In this chapter and the next one, our focus will be on brushing up the technical details for REST API. For the most part, some of the info here might not be truly useful for a professional looking just to build apps, but it can serve usefully if you want to learn more about REST API in depth.

We will try to follow the rise and growth as well as the usefulness of REST API here.

Ever since the release of REST API, it being at its 1.2 version of development as we write, there has been much excitement from developers regarding it. The JSON API plugin is among the key things to be incorporated in the core, but since it is proving to be bigger than expected, full integration is awaited. The challenges the developer team is facing are immense, and it will take a lot of time and effort until a *universal API* is built.

Backward compatibility

Backward compatibility has been one of the main tasks, ever since the release of the first version of the plugin, and the developers behind it are trying to be committed to this aim. The second version, which will be merged into the core, is not going to provide full backward compatibility, but at least the plugin will continue to exist as a backward-compatibility layer that will allow any plugin that was developed in the plugin's first version with the ability to function properly.

It is obvious that developers are not going to be recreating the plugin from scratch and would rather be porting things over from the first version to the second one.

Thus, the routes will have to be prefixed, and the core will make use of a `wp` prefix, and all of the custom routes will be assigned their prefixes. The `wp-JSON` prefix that is currently used for routes is most likely not going to be used, and instead websites that will be using the plugin are going to get the old WP-JSON routes rerouted to their new routes as long as they're within the core.

Another idea set by developers is that anyone will be able to make good use of the plugin, and the compatibility layer will make it look very similar to the earlier version of the plugin, which is regarded as a fixed point in this sense. It, however, will make use of its second version and the core infrastructure so the key point in this is that the code written for version 1 will immediately benefit from all the bug fixes that are there and still have security maintenance that will avoid supporting two versions at the same time.

A universal API

Another aim is to create a universal API, given all the advancement of the REST API plugin. When developers were asked about this, they stated that one of the biggest concerns out there is the difficulty of creating a perfect balance, as adding default endpoints in the core has a lot of complexity in terms of ensuring the correct data is in the proper place. Another thing to set is that the balance varies, competing concerns might sometimes arise, and in that case it represents a major challenge, which is why its development might take more time than expected.

Another interesting point is that creating such an API will allow the further creation of frontend websites by someone who doesn't know how to develop for WordPress, which will expand its horizons in terms of how development for the **Content Management System** (**CMS**) will evolve.

Another interesting case is the prediction of how WordPress-powered mobile applications will evolve. In such cases, the primary goal is to make the API work as a consistent piece across all existing websites, which creates an expectation that is impossible to fulfill, the provision of data from every site. Most of these problems will probably be very hard to handle, given how many apparent inconsistencies there are amongst such an outrageous amount of websites. The correct aim here is the balance that is being tried to achieve, which will allow plugin developers the right flexibility and strictness expected by clients.

Architectural structure

The architectural properties and constraints set by the REST architectural style is divided into several parts, such as scalability, which is meant to provide proper support for a numerous amount of significant components and interactions between components, the main effect on scalability being considered as follows:

- Performance is another key component that acts on the interactions which play a significant role in user-perceived performance and network efficiency
- Components are bound to modifications that meet changing needs, including when the application runs
- Portable components by a moving program code with the data
- System level resistance at failure, which assures reliability and in the presence of failures within components or data, prevention plays its role
- Simple, efficient and transparent interfaces

The separation between concerns will create simpler component implementation and thus will reduce the complexity in the connector semantics, which will then improve the effectiveness and the performance tuning of the server components.

In a layered system, such constraints will allow intermediaries such as proxies, gateways and firewalls to be introduced at various points in the communication without needing to change the available interfaces between components, which will lead to the possibility of communicating without having any issue in communication translation and performance improvement by making good use of large-scale shared caching and will positively affect the caching.

REST architectural constraints

The properties of architecture within REST are realized by applying specific interactions, which will constrain to components, connectors and data elements that can describe applications that are conforming to REST constraints such as RESTful. If any of these constraints are not met, then the application can no longer be considered as a RESTful one. If the compliance with these limitations is achieved, which would be the equivalent of conforming to the REST architectural style, then the system will have non-functional properties such as scalability and performance, simplicity, and portability with further reliability. Under this section, we will cover the formal, known REST constraints in detail.

The formal REST constraints

There are a few formal REST constraints that we will get to know briefly, as follows:

- Stateless
- Client-server
- Layered system
- Cacheable
- Code on demand
- Uniform interfaces
- Self descriptive messages

Stateless

The client-server communication is further restricted by the absence of any client context that would store data between requests on the server. Any request that will be passed will contain in it all the required information to service the request, and thus the sessions state that will be held within the client. The state of a session, that is going to be transferred by the server to any other service such as the database to maintain a continuous state, will allow further authentication. The client will then start to send requests when it is ready to pass to a transition that will allow this authentication. When the client starts sending such requests, it is the appropriate time to make a move to a new state, and while requests are outstanding, the client will be considered to be in the process of a transition. Any consecutive initiation of state-transition will permit the use of links contained in the application state.

Client-server

An interface that is uniform will separate the client from the server, which would mean that clients are not concerned with data storage of any kind, and remain internal to each other in a way that means the portability of the client code is improved. At this stage, servers are not bothered with user interface or state, which makes them a lot simpler and more flexible towards scalability. The servers and clients can also be replaced and developed independently as long as the interface between them is not altered in any way.

Layered system

The tiered system that is in place implies that a client cannot tell in an ordinary manner whether it is connected directly to the end server or via an intermediary method. The intermediary solution comes to improve system's scalability by enabling balance load and making use of shared caches that can further imply different security policies.

Cacheable

Clients and intermediaries will cache responses in a manner that must implicitly or explicitly suggest a definition in themselves as cacheable that is going to prevent clients from reusing any inappropriate data in response to further requests. Good management of the cache will wholly or partially eliminate any client-server interaction that will affect performance and scalability in a positive way.

Code on demand

Servers can make use of temporary extensions or customizations that will affect the functionality of a client in the transfer of executable code that is an optional constraint of the REST architecture.

Uniform interfaces

A uniform interface constraint is one of the basics of the design in a REST service in that the uniform interface will simplify and decouple the architecture, which will then enable each part of it independently, it being divided into few more consistent interfaces, which are:

- Resource identification
- Representation and resources

We will have brief information about these two parameters as follows:

Resource identification

Individual resources are identified within requests, and for this we will be using URLs in web-based REST systems that in themselves are separate representations of conceptions that are then returned to the client. An example of this is data sending by the server in a format that does not correspond to the internal representation of the server.

Representation and resources

When there is a client that holds within itself a representation of a resource, including but not limited to paired metadata, then it is considered that there's enough data to apply any modifications to the resource.

Self-descriptive messages

There's sufficient information included within each of the messages, allowing us to receive a description of how to process the messages, which can involve a parser to invoke it that may be specified by an Internet media type file.

HATEOS

Hypermedia As The Engine Of Application State (**HATEOS**) states, for the hypermedia as the engine of the application state, that clients make state transitions only through actions that are considered to be dynamically identified in a hypermedia by the server and, except for a simple fixed entry points to the application, a client should not make the assumption that any action, in particular, is available for any individual resource that is beyond those that have been described in a representation that has been previously received from the server.

Ever-growing REST API

While work on REST API has started, the development of the project has since taken an extended period because of the aim the project has nowadays—growing exponentially. In the beginning, the REST API was just a method of underlying data in WordPress, and some of the code found in the first version still exists nowadays. The limit is set at four core objects such as the users, posts, taxonomies and metadata that were decided early on. Even if this seems somewhat set on limitations, it will set the REST API to cover options and any other kind of data types. The REST API, being identical to the core of WordPress, was built with extensibility in mind and thus includes the infrastructure for handling the remaining data types in doing anything that you'd like as a developer.

The infrastructure of the API will support nearly everything, and if the core endpoints are taken away, it will be considered as a framework for building APIs that can be built any way you'd like. It, however, is not going to solve all issues that there might be, but would rather come as a supplement to the current technical advances and flexibility in such a manner and regard. The REST API will not satisfy the need WordPress has for a generic API.

To achieve this, developers would like to allow such flexibility to plugin developers, who have to understand that when they're granted the desired flexibility there's a downside as well, which might be the misuse that can result in removed endpoints and broken applications.

Overall, this comes to work as a perfect API for millions of websites that work in different ways. At this point, the REST API provides a fully-functional solution that is ready for anyone to use, with all the power needed for site and plugin developers to easily customize.

REST API as a platform

The REST API at its 1.2.3 version adds some extensibility to the already flexible and robust CMS that WordPress is considered to be. It provides the benefit of turning WordPress into an entirely innovative application framework that will further adapt to custom data types while still maintaining a natural note and way of maintaining. The REST API is meant to not interfere with new data types and thus will not break them when any protocol is changed. An API such as REST will let us extend the possibilities that we already have regarding usage of WordPress and progress in its development.

REST, which is defined as the **Representational State Transfer,** uses the HTTP connection to offer some advantages to WordPress, such as the ability to interact with more objects and verbs, reuse interfaces no matter what the native protocol, such as JSON, and then provide integration with various plugins. The stability and scalability of the framework also provides more options regarding data type changing and the way new application interfaces are developed.

It is to be understood that any application depends on the top of an operating system, which has got to be implemented in pair with the API, after which the gathered data from local storage is converted by the application and will regard pre-determined protocols, rules, and procedures. Specific APIs are designed to interact with particular kinds of objects, which are hypermedia data objects, that interact in the memory pool of the following code specifications (`PUT`, `GET`, `DELETE`) and security methods such as `OAuth` and `SSL`.

A thing to set is that REST is different from other web application interfaces in the way the objects are found in memory, as it does not put any constraint on the way the strict data rules and definitions are set. Another point is that REST will eliminate any need to build different APIs for each new project created, and also provides better improvement in extensibility and future possible protocol changes.

REST itself is an interface that has no referenced links to other old protocols, which is why we can have easy data shifts from any earlier hypertext focus to a newer one, this setting the basis for future improvement as protocols and definitions change over time. REST will parse a broad range of programming languages without any preconceptions, and it will probably work as a solution that provides frequent interaction between your legacy pages and your WordPress site. Another thing to notice is that thanks to REST developers can now consider REST as a solution for applying the same operations to more open-ended objects that will not result in technical issues or to them not functioning at all.

Implementing REST API in apps

One more thing to say is that the RESTful API manifests itself as the application framework that it already is. The first point would be the taxonomies to custom post types transition, which would provide code modifications upon activation that will give you the possibility to create user-defined post types with their own taxonomies, which would only provide changes to the WordPress core files. As was assessed before, REST API is only working its way up to being implemented in the core of WordPress, and is not yet a completed implementation.

Custom data types in WordPress

Another thing to notice is the transition from a CMS towards an Application framework, which provides the typical WordPress CMS framework in applications with customized data types, all this being achieved by the extended features of REST and its capability in terms of specifications, protocols, and technologies like JSON and AJAX. The working version of **WP-REST-API v.2.0** might come in useful for some testing purposes, but given its state, which is currently in production, considering it for installment on a production website is not a good idea.

REST API is not to be considered a feature of the typical WordPress CMS with its standard features and requests. It is more of a developer tool that is meant to provide flexible and secure content management, but with more specialized and advanced needs. A reliable framework is the primary necessity of every user, and REST API improves the reliability or performance in this regard, making it a worthwhile measure with respect to development and application pairing to WordPress. The REST API will additionally provide better functionality and a stronger basis for application development, and installing such APIs will grant the chance of accommodating further protocols, given the flexibility they are built with.

REST API in later versions of WordPress

REST API within later versions of WordPress will provide the possibility of being able to use the second version of the infrastructure of the API that is now a part of the core in WordPress. The activation will lead to a REST API for the content of your site and will expose your data in a JSON format. The response data that you will receive is going to be similar to what you would get in the WordPress loop, with the sole difference being the format, which is JSON, which will allow display in any way, and can even filter the API calls in a similar manner to the loop.

We shall assess the fact that some API calls are going to require authentication and, just like WordPress required authentication to get access to `wp-admin` or to create a new post, most GET requests will not require authentication and will allow content to be displayed via the API to a third-party external app without requiring a credentials request for the user.

WordPress is the content management system of preference for many people because it is easy to add new content types to it, and another crucial benefit of the JSON API is how it will work with the custom post types, which will require a new type parameter to the API request to be accessed. Custom metadata is not going to be added for you, and if you would like to include some custom metadata it would be relatively easy to do it with a set filter.

Most of the API endpoints and post JSON responses are filtered out by using the `get_posts` functions. To add metadata to a post, a post request would be sent to supply a value within the data parameter and calls of the authenticated API would be performed to `PUT` or `DELETE` content.

Whether you question why you would need a JSON API in WordPress or not, the fact that it allows access to data without any constraints remains, and thus permits those developers who make use of it to create applications that will have custom and advanced functionality, making it possible to access your website's data without having to reload the entire page. Overall, great experiences can be created for both developers and end users when there's a similar API data structure running on a multitude of websites.

REST API and WordPress plugin development

Under this section of our chapter, we will discuss how REST API is going to, or has already, influenced developers that revolve around WordPress, whose livings rely on building plugins, themes, and so on. WordPress, being a massively used content management system, has specific requirements and constantly growing needs given its constant improvement.

The API requirements have to be placed first when thinking development-wise, as the interaction of a plugin as the client is going to rely more on the API and such.

REST API routes are PHP code that has to have a stable and functional code. The real potential of default routes within REST API potentially can be as a repurposed **Software as a Service** (**SAAS**) service.

The REST API will make a dependency injection regarding class design, and backward compatibility will probably arise for older plugins. These plugins have to deal with backward compatibility issues, and existing plugins might require some improvement of the code if they want to work with REST API. Plugins that will not commit to such an improvement will risk their very existence, mainly because their functionality might be put in question in a further version of WordPress. Easier interfaces and better experiences will make it easier to build WordPress as an ever-growing content management system.

REST API-based authentication

Among the several options that are available for authenticating with the API, the primary choice will cover one of these two options:

- For a mobile, web or desktop client, that will be accessing the site externally, you will be using the OAuth method of authentication with the application of passwords or basic authentication
- For themes or plugins that are running on a site, you will be making use of the cookie authentication method.

In the following sections, we will try to cover both of the options and their particulars.

OAuth authentication

The OAuth authentication method is the primary handler in authentication that is used for any external clients, making it go through the steps of a standard authentication and then authorizing the clients to act on their behalf, which are then issued with corresponding OAuth tokens that will give them access to the API that is revocable by the users at any time.

Once the WP API and the OAuth server plugins are activated on your server, all you will have to do is create a `client` that will work as an identifier for the application itself, which will then include.

After you activate the OAuth and WP API plugin on your server, create a `client` that it represents and an identifier for the application which will include a `key` and `secret` that will both need a link to your website. The OAuth server plugin will now have a full admin user-interface and will include a client application management and the ability to revoke tokens. To generate a new client application, you should notice an `Applications` item somewhere under the users menu where the OAuth clients are managed.

Basic authentication

Basic authentication is one of the optional handlers of authentication for external clients. Given the complexity system of the OAuth authentication, a basic one can be useful during development. It, however, will require the pass of credentials with each request and will then provide them to clients, which makes it profoundly discouraged for mass usage.

Application passwords are used similarly, the difference being that you don't have to provide a normal account password and you would rather be provided with a unique revocable password that will be generated within WordPress admin. These passwords are only available for the REST API, and its legacy of the XML-RPC API could not necessarily be used to log into WordPress. Authentication and application passwords require installation of either the application passwords plugin or the basic auth one, which would need a pass of the username with each request that is passed through the `Authorization` header.

Cookie authentication

The authentication method makes use of cookies the primary method included within WordPress. This makes it so the cookies are set up correctly when you log in to your dashboard, so that developers of plugins and themes only need the user to be logged in. This is true, yet the REST API will make use of a technique called **nonces,** which will help to avoid **Cross-site Request Forgery** (**CSRF**) issues. This will provide you with the possibility of avoiding other sites to perform actions without needing to explicitly intend to do this, which would require a kind of different way of handling the API.

Developers using the built-in JavaScript API will not have any issues in this regard; this is mainly recommended for use relating to the API in plugins and themes. Using `wp.api.models.Base` will extend the assurance that correct data is being sent for any custom requests.

Nonce will be needed to pass with each request in the case of manual Ajax requests, which would then make the API use nonces with the action set to `wp_rest`. Further passage to the API will be performed via the data parameter of `_wpnonce` (`POST` data or the query for `GET` requests) via the `X-WP-Nonce` header. One thing to assess is that supplying the nonce as a header is probably the most reliable approach available at the moment, given that PHP doesn't transform the request body of a `DELETE` request into a super global one.

The cookie authentication method relies strictly on WordPress cookies, which is why this method will only be suitable when the REST API is used inside WordPress and the current user is logged in within the system. Additionally, the user has got to have a corresponding capability to perform the action.

REST API and security

As we have previously mentioned, the infrastructure of WordPress will be included within the core of WordPress itself in version 4.4. The release of the upcoming WordPress version will yield several endpoints for the REST API, which has brought up some debates regarding how security will be handled.

REST, being the stateless client-server protocol that it is, will be used over HTTP most of the time. REST is not a specific API for WordPress, and is mostly used for non-specific tasks over the web as a standard protocol. The WordPress REST API will make your website a web service that applications will be able to retrieve data from, and all this will happen on an automated basis with no need to access the website from the browser.

Regarding how the WordPress REST API works, we will retrieve information from a website that works as a target. This will send a specific HTTP GET request that will be further conducted to the REST API. Your target website will not return any data that is not already available publicly; it, however, will return an easy to understand format for the APIs which can then send over other requests.

One thing to state is that anyone can query the WordPress API on your WordPress powered website, and by this they can retrieve public info such as comments, pages, and posts. Another method of use is to update and retrieve information regarding users or posts, yet such tasks will only be achieved if an authentication is performed. The API will allow similar functionality to a normal WordPress and is going to provide an install with no need for any user-friendly interface, given the level at which these queries, requests and operations are performed.

As an overall appreciation of security, it is to be admitted that the WordPress API might or might not pose new security risks, which will be looked over. Overall, the only security concern is the fact that the REST API, just like any API, represents a risk in itself because it is an additional attack surface on WordPress, and the more attack surfaces there are, the broader the chances for hackers to exploit or take advantage. In this regard it shall be mentioned that no particular vulnerability within REST API has been found, so we are now facing more of a *generic* or common security concern rather than something specific about the REST API. Another thing to be mentioned is that the REST API will only make use of the information that is publicly available, which other services like an RSS or the front-end of the website itself would have access to, so you shouldn't look at REST as if it's an incredibly innovative yet unknown thing in regard to how it works.

Overall, it should be considered that REST API is a secure and tested solution that is used by millions, which is why if you keep up general maintenance of your site with timely updates, for example, then no worries regarding security will concern you. As we have looked at already, the upcoming changes to the REST API will provide developers with a bigger pool of options for development choices and possibilities, which is always only a good thing.

REST API being used in WordPress plugins

REST API, being considered as an ever-growing and reliable solution, has become the backbone for a multitude of WordPress plugins that offer a wide range of functionality from contact forms to menus and means of authentication. This proves that the future lies on REST API, and developers have actively started making use of it.

Under this section, we will cover the Thermal API plugin, one of the main plugins built with REST API.

Overview

Thermal API will allow you to elevate your WordPress content in a very familiar WordPress manner. Thermal is the plugin that will give you the power of `WP_QUERY` in a RESTful API way. Thermal will support client-based decisions and has a responsive design framework that is going to allow for a responsive application that will leverage a WordPress content source.

Thermal will be considered as a gateway between your WordPress-managed content and its consumption. Thermal will expose your content for a variety of uses such as native applications, syndication, embeds and mobile web interfaces. It will help you use your WordPress content from anywhere, however you would like. Thermal will be particularly useful if you are working with mobile applications or syndication networks. It will set your WordPress-managed content, which will be free between numerous devices and platforms that will let you do that with an interface that works and acts like you are expecting WordPress to work.

These are the main reasons that you should consider regarding WordPress:

- Thermal makes use of REST, so it follows the usual URL structure of other web APIs
- Thermal will use the exact query parameters such as `WP_Query`, and there is no need to learn a new syntax
- Thermal relies on top of WordPress' internal APIs where caching is assured
- Thermal is provided with active maintenance
- Thermal automatically supports all public custom post types and taxonomies.

To get started with Thermal, all you will have to do is download the plugin and then go into the documentation. We will bypass that info, since it is beyond the scope of this book. Because Thermal is a new API, it is yet to gain high popularity.

Disabling REST API

We have assessed, using numerous instances, the benefits of REST API and how it is progressing, and we have also looked over the security concerns that might be bothering you. In this regard, we will look over the practical method to disable the JSON REST API in WordPress.

Some website owners might not be using all the features provided by the API, and if they are skeptical about the security concerns that revolve around REST, and you would like to secure themself from a DDoS attack, then similarly to disabling **Extensible Markup Language-Remote Procedure Call Protocol** (**XML-RPC**), you could disable the REST API.

To disable the JSON REST API on your WordPress website, you will have to add a piece of code within the `functions.php` file of your theme files.

```
add_filter('json_enabled', '__return_false');
add_filter('json_jsonp_enabled', '__return_false');
```

The code piece above will make use of the available built-in filters, which will then disable the JSON and JSONP APIs. To manually add the code, you will have to install and then activate the disable JSON API plugin, which will work out of the box with no settings required for you to configure.

Summary

We have now covered the details of REST API, its background, and the larger role that it can play in your WordPress projects. Our next and final stop will deal with all the remaining coverage of REST API, and summarizing its usability for WP developers.

8
WordPress REST API in Practice

WordPress is, step by step, becoming an application framework, which implies the need for APIs that will allow new functionality. The REST API plugin is the physical manifestation through which the REST API will be used, its functionality being described in brief would be the retrieval of users, posts, taxonomies and other server-side data that by the means of this plugin will be achieved more easily. WP API will provide a simple and standard interface to the WP Query, the APIs of posts, users and post meta, which also includes an alternative API based on Backbone models that provides developers of WordPress themes and plugins with the possibility to get up and running, and retrieve data without knowing any details about how to connect to the said server.

This chapter will give you a crash course in WordPress REST API itself. Yes, the API itself. There is not much coding here, but if you need thorough background info about REST API in WordPress, this is the chapter to read.

WordPress REST API is currently at its second version, and it is important to state that a few key changes have been applied to the second version of the plugin, which we will go through now.

Key differences between v1 and v2 of the plugin

The stage of development of the second version of the plugin is now at the beta 1 of v2, and while the developers team believes that the API is stable enough to be used in public testing, they admit that they could still occasionally break it in order to have it further improved, thus it is strongly suggested you only use the API in development contexts and avoid production environments for version 2 of the plugin.

Internal changes

Endpoints will take a single parameter, as opposed to the previous version. The endpoint in question is `WP_REST_Request`. The argument registration has been transferred to route registration, and argument options are set to a default value.

- `Register_rest_route` will now help with route registration, but requires the use of a namespace. It is used with the plugin slug along the plugin version like so `wp/v2`.
- Built-in endpoints will now make use of a typical controller base class, which has its standardized pattern. In version 2, this changed to become a public API for developers, and the recommendation is that this is applied when working with most use cases. While it is not mandatory in custom code, it will just embody best practices in the core of the API.
- Callbacks with permissions will now be registered in a separate manner towards the response callback, which will allow better capability assertions for clients.
- The server will now sanitize and validate arguments for us by making use of `validate_callback` and `sanitize_callback` options at the time of registering arguments. The callback for validation will then return truth values for valid parameters, false ones for invalid parameters and errors respectively.

External changes

The external changes performed are as follows:

- The core routes within WordPress have been transferred to the `wp/v2` namespace.

- To follow the **Hypertext Application Language** (**HAL**) standards, the hypermedia links have been changed from `meta.links` to `_links`.
- Links will be given an embeddable attribute that will indicate whether they can or cannot be embedded within the response.
- Defined content types will have a schema attributed to the endpoint in a way that will follow the JSON Schema standard
- Comments have also suffered a change in the way that they have been moved to a top-level endpoint in the manner of `/wp/v2/comments`.

Future changes

There are expected future changes for the API, which would go beyond the second beta of the plugin. Those changes would cover:

- Auto-validation for schemes and improvement to their internal and external use
    - User meta access
    - Links from collections
    - Public user access to the data for authors
- Improved handling of how deleting is covered

Functions of APIs

APIs are sets of protocols and routines that are used within building applications for PCs, web or services. An API will specify the necessary interaction that is occurring within components; it mainly provides a foundation for building an application. In short, the API will help with sharing data between programs and thus improve interaction. The API will provide access to the internal functions of applications so that other third-party software or services can make use of this functionality. Most of the time, by the means of an API, the developers are being provided with access to major services that provide some sort of functionality, which is then used by developers to build even more extensive apps on top of the primary ones, thus an open yet secure form of collaboration is occurring between the parties involved.

The REST API in theory

The Representational State Transfer, which stands for REST, is an architectural style of API that is intended to provide a lightweight form of communication between the parties (**consumer** and **producer**) and thus create an optimal solution for services with a high volume of operation like the WordPress CMS.

By combining an architectural style of REST and JSON, the WP API is composed, which yields a great tool used by developers that can share data from their WordPress websites to other applications or services. The WP API will allow the actions of creating, reading, updating, and deleting data from a site, specifically posts, users, pages, media, comments, and so on. Overall all kinds of possible content can be manipulated by using the WP API.

The WP API, being in its second version, is now a preferred method of development by many. JavaScript based functionality will be the first aim, and through this opening large room for operation for the said API, specifically content editing, validation of forms, and operations relating to themes and plugins that are based on JavaScript. Content manipulation in specific opens a lot of creative solutions within development possibilities, thus promoting new development techniques, solving current problems and getting rid of limitations that might still exist.

As WordPress is moving towards becoming a fully-fledged application framework, REST API comes to prove the amount of control developers and users have been given with regard to the content management system. New content experiences will now be built thanks to this plugin, given the possibility of managing the content of a WordPress-powered website from an application other than the official one. Third-party applications could also be used in some other form with regard to your content, be that a new form of integration of apps within your site, or your content within other applications, it is still a new step forward for how we perceive content operations and development possibilities overall.

The future of WordPress is also strongly tied to how we will utilize the functionality of WP API, and it is believed that once the plugin gets out of the beta production state, its use will proportionally increase. As WordPress has a broader use, the ways we will be making applications interact with it will also increase, thus more interesting and creative approaches will appear.

A guide to HTTP and REST

REST is a simple and easy way to assign interactions that happen between systems. It has been implemented more and more within APIs, all because REST has a minimal overhead regarding clients of all kinds (desktop computers, mobile phones, online services). REST, being inspired by HTTP, is a system that is used either in pair with it or more likely in places where you would make use of HTTP. It is considered that REST has a strong pair with HTTP, given that building on top of HTTP requires the use of XML-based languages like SOAP, which has totally different conventions and still has limitations. While making use of SOAP is indeed useful in some particular scenarios, when working with HTTP it is a better idea to refer to REST, given that it has been built upon it.

HTTP

HTTP is the protocol that allows the transfer of documents and data on the web by determining exchanged messages that are appropriate to reply to others. The HTTP relies on two roles, the server, and the client. The client will initiate the conversation and then a related reply from the server will follow up. The messages within HTTP are text ones. Thus they are either pieces of text and media of some types. The messages of HTTP are divided into bodies and headers. The bodies will contain within themselves data that could be sent over the network, yet they could also remain empty. The header will contain metadata and the HTTP methods when this is requested. Contrary to this, REST will apply more importance to the header data rather than the body.

The HTTP client and server will exchange information about identified resources by making use of URLs. It is stated that the request and responses will contain a representation of the resources, meaning a certain format regarding the state of the resource and how that state should be in the future, including the pieces of representation that are the body and the header.

The metadata is contained within HTTP headers and thus are tied by the specs of HTTP. The body will then hold data in any formats and further send the media through requests on metadata or different URLs. Applications are usually built in a manner that will change the format of the data and then tailor themselves for various clients and preferences.

HTTP client libraries

To have the possibility of working with different request methods, you will need to have a client that allows you to specify a method of use. As APIs are accessed by using a separate client application, or the browser, it is important to have decent capabilities of the HTTP client within the programming language you choose to work with. The HTTP client library you would most likely make use of would be `curl`, which includes a library that can be used by the majority of programming languages and also includes a standalone command line program.

The HTTP protocol was made up to provide a mean of communication between systems which would have as their common point the way they perceive the protocol. When working with REST and HTTP, it is a good idea not to use PHP but rather use Ruby or Python with their corresponding frameworks, as their support for REST is better.

The WordPress REST API

The WordPress REST API is a huge breakthrough in the evolutionary process of WordPress as a CMS from one side, and as a fully-fledged application framework from another side. We will try to cover most of the features and practical uses of this API so that there aren't any unclear points left behind. At this very stage, the REST API has undergone a thorough evolution phase from being just an idea supported by one person to a global API that is considered to make it within the core in the nearest future, it being backed up not only a solid team of developers constantly working on improving it but also by its separate mini-community within the larger WordPress one.

The JSON REST API

The JSON REST API will now make it possible to manipulate and use code to ease up trivial tasks like creating content and working with posts, pages and users with minimal effort. The interface that was created by the core team makes it an easy and undaunting task.

JSON, the JavaScript Object Notation, is a preferred format for creating structures that will then be used by our data, and thus applications will be able to make good use of it. JSON-formatted data can be created from one programming language and then processed from another, thus making communication between systems and languages way easier through a common data format, which JSON is. This opens the room for a proper expansion of how we perceive WordPress now and in the closest future.

REST, the Representational State Transfer, is an architectural preference that relies on HTTP and thus has as its primary actions POST, GET, PUT and DELETE. In short, we now make manipulations of data by using HTTP and relying on REST API.

Rest API would be considered so because it has a set of defined aspects, like the basic URI, standard HTTP methods (GET/PUT/POST/DELETE), hypertext links that have reference to the state and related resources, and an internet media type like JSON or XML.

The WordPress REST API is an interface for common data and programming that writes and reads information from the WordPress applications as we used to know them. Regarding the use of REST API, it is pretty obvious that its main purpose will cover data reading and manipulations, including within third party applications.

Because of the functionality of REST API, we will now go beyond the common means of writing, editing, retrieving and deleting data. This will be covered regarding the so-common front-end of the WordPress we have been used to using with regard to data manipulations. Now, we will only need to have access to the backend to successfully complete actions of these kinds. Custom APIs could and are already used to accomplish the very same result, yet custom APIs impose more restrictions and are way limited compared to a global, core-integrated plugin, as REST API is about to become. It also imposes limitations for the millions of users who do not have such custom-built APIs built. Because the admin page will no longer be such a big necessity, applications of all kinds will pop up and the importance put on the need to perform from the frontend will reduce.

Integrating applications with WordPress will become an even easier task than it is now as the old way of pairing used to be by using XML-RPC. Now, with the REST API set in place, the ability to allow and perform complex functions is way higher. The REST API will also give the possibility of having direct communication with the database.

Developers of WP REST API

With the development of the REST API, and its incorporation within the core of WordPress, it is pretty obvious that an end result like the said plugin requires a lot of work and effort, with somebody being responsible for it.

Ryan McCue, the person behind the WordPress core, started contributing to the community more than five years ago, and he is now the person responsible for creating the JSON REST API, which is a platform that is very easy to work with and that can easily interact with any programming language and thus benefit any program with an API access, including support for a native iOS and Android system. Even if the development goes on, improved website experiences are already resulting from this API as it leaves behind several restrictions that current APIs impose. Matt Mullenweg, the main guy behind WordPress, also considers that as WordPress continues to evolve, a bigger focus from the application standpoint will be created once the API is implemented within the core. Functionalities like infinite scroll and live reloading are already starting to become basics even for official WordPress themes, and the flexibility of such APIs, compared to a more complicated system like XML-RPC, solves a lot of issues and hassles.

Overall description

From an overall point of view, the REST API is a great innovation within the WordPress development community, mainly because of its great features that permit content to be saved from other apps and websites no matter if they use WordPress, and by this, thoroughly extending the capabilities that WordPress currently has. By using the REST API, developers will build new applications for site management and content editing that will be something much different than the current admin panel located within WordPress.

Plugin and template developers will be able to do their job more easily, given that plugins and themes will be able to load the content dynamically, and in this way a more standardized way of handling AJAX from the frontend will become a norm.

The RESTful API, which remains the basis of the REST API, is also considered to overcome the limitations that the current technology of the XML-RPC API imposes, regarding how requests and responses are made. Thus the usage of JSON within the REST API will interact better with the majority of programming languages as well.

In this way, we will no longer perceive WordPress as a content management tool alone, and will look at it more as a new way of interacting with any data within WordPress such as users, posts, and media. While the usages of REST API within WordPress are broad and useful, the way it will find its use in other third-party applications such as mobile applications is even more pleasantly surprising. The dynamicity and extensiveness of plugins and themes that can result from making use of the REST API will also be pretty great. It is to be considered that WordPress will benefit greatly from the REST API, as it will only increase the demand for the CMS, considering that it will no longer be perceived as a CMS alone given the technical possibilities surrounding it.

Considering the momentum that REST API has been gaining in the last three years, it now no longer represents a simple plugin but more of a fascinating solution for thousands of developers who have been forced to make use of less functional, **hassle-full** methods when working with WordPress. The fact that a generic API will be added to all those websites that are powered out there sounds like an impossible mission, yet it has been proven that even if it's hard, progress will continue, and REST API is definitely the next cool thing about

WordPress and everything surrounding it. One more thing, is that given the constantly increasing popularity and demand, developers will start paying more attention to it and considering it for possible implementation of their projects. That's impressive progress, considering the unimportance everyone was assigning to this plugin when just one single developer was behind it, and not even he imagined such a fast core integration for his product.

JSON

JSON, as in JavaScript Object Notation, is an open-standard format that makes use of readable text to send data objects made of attribute value pairs. It is considered to be the main alternative XML and is the most common data format used for the communication between browsers-servers.

The JSON format data is available in many programming languages and because of the common conventions with other programming languages like C, Java, and Python, it is a perfect language for data interchanging.

JSON has two structures as its fundamentals:

- A list of values that will be realized as arrays, vectors, lists or sequences
- A collection of value pairs that will be realized as objects, associative arrays, and so on.

Given the universality of these data structures, most modern programming languages can easily support them in one form or another, and thus create easy interchangeable data formats between languages that are also based on these structures. The JSON lies at the foundation of REST API, and has become famous for the fact that by the REST API, and thus JSON, a lot of new functionality will be brought to WordPress, such as:

- Client-side applications powered by WordPress
- Form processing using AJAX and the JSON REST API
- Improved metadata sorting by REST API

JavaScript

JavaScript, as an ever-growing language used for front-end development, has started to gather more and more popularity in the last year and has now started to cross lines with WordPress. Whenever Matt Mullenweg himself throws a suggestion stating that it's worth it for WordPress developers to learn JavaScript, something interesting is going to come our way. While WordPress mainly consists of its Codex and PHP for fundamentals, JavaScript does have a few similarities with them, so it is worth taking the opportunity to start learning the language given the rise of how it is going to be implemented within themes and plugins and its interaction with the WP REST API.

JavaScript, as a front-end language used for development, does a client-side communication with the browser of the user who's visiting your website, while PHP does the server-side communication. It is more than likely that you're acquainted with these notions, yet have you ever thought about how JavaScript could improve the overall experience when compared to PHP, especially by limiting those server requests sent by PHP. As we're all about progress and improvement, speed has always been a concern and alternatives to PHP as the backbone of WordPress could pop up faster than we might expect.

JavaScript has its downsides as well, as there's no ideal or perfect solution and more of a perfect individual choice. The same goes for JavaScript: if you actually want those server requests to happen, then you're out of luck. Also, there are some small concerns about how JavaScript will interact with older browsers and thus compatibility might be brought up as a reason not to consider JavaScript.

While the preceding text might sound a little bit pragmatic, it's a fact that JavaScript is already a big part of WordPress and that manifests in the presence of JSON and jQuery within it, along with a bunch of other JavaScript libraries that are present. Our main concern in this topic is the interaction of JSON with the WP REST API, but that will be looked at in a minute.

The biggest use of JavaScript within WordPress, besides the libraries lying at its base, is the WordPress Admin panel, which couldn't be any more essential, at least for the time being. Again, I believe its importance will drop drastically once the WP REST API starts taking huge turnovers, but for time being, it still stays as the **frontend core** part of WordPress. All changes on the admin screen are done by means of JavaScript, the only exception being those changes that cover the server-side actions of CRUD: Creating, Updating or Deleting posts.

JavaScript within WordPress is heavily used in the majority of those themes and plugins that are present on your website and are responsible for the effects of sliders and dynamic effects.

And to end the showcase of where JavaScript is used within WordPress, it should be stated that the WP REST API is a clear example of how JavaScript gets to interact with WordPress. The JSON objects would be used, thus granting interaction of JavaScript with the database. This changes a lot, given how close we are getting to a full interaction of JavaScript with WordPress.

The only difficulty in the way of JavaScript taking over the lead position for powering WordPress is PHP, which is definitely a brave opponent. Overall, there are quite a few familiar concepts found both in PHP and JavaScript that are helpful when learning either one of those two. The main common points within JavaScript and PHP would be the syntax (which has both common and distinct points), variables, operators, comments, strings, arrays and functions.

WP REST API and JavaScript

The biggest advance of JavaScript in the WordPress field is the WP REST API, which lets you do some backend magic such as interacting with the site database. JSON is responsible for doing the backend actions of editing, writing and reading data by following JavaScript concepts that lie at its foundation. Using JSON within the REST API would require you to use an HTTP client, which will allow the interaction to happen between the API and client. You will proceed to authenticate to your site, but one requirement is to have REST API enabled, which on WordPress sites is set as active, by default. In case you're not sure whether REST API is enabled or not, you should take a look through the official REST API documentation to choose one of the available methods. Authentication will happen either by OAuth authentication, cookie authentication or an active plugin or theme on the site. The next step is to fetch, edit and post data, which will end up with manipulating the said data—the main feature of WP REST API. The possibilities for avoiding PHP entirely or mixing up PHP and JavaScript definitely open up the room for a lot of possible combinations and development experiments.

XML-RPC in WordPress

XML-RPC is the remote protocol, which uses XML in order to encode the calls as a transport method, which has caused a bit of a trouble within the WordPress community and to the platform itself. The interface is said to be insecure given its bad means of encryption and sending plain usernames and passwords in its requests. And it is known to be sending quite a few requests in order to access your site, and with every access, especially when browsing over unsecured HTTP connections, your credentials are put at risk. The risk of hacking has brought up several WordPress plugins that have the intention of providing a new method of authentication that wouldn't put your credentials at risk. These plugins work by creating secret keys within the XML documents and then passing them through the Authorization header when sending the request to WordPress.

The preceding approach is more of an optimistic way to look at how the things are without ditching the XML-RPC solution of remotely connecting to a site altogether, yet there's a different option that also has the right to be considered. That would be to admit that XML-RPC is a vulnerable and inconsistent solution that works but creates too many vulnerabilities such that at times developers would even refer to it as a Pyrrhic victory (a victory which inflicts a devastating toll upon the winner) given how many websites have been exploited, hacked and attacked by the means of XML-RPC.

An interesting thought has been flowing on the Web stating that security plugins for XML-RPC are not helpful, simply because the users who are having their websites hacked are precisely the ones who wouldn't make use of such a plugin, which really makes us look at this concern in a different fashion. XML-RPC, with the provided functionality of remotely connecting to websites, has definitely been usable, and actually used by the Jetpack plugin and mobile applications. But with the previously mentioned concerns and the WP REST API, which is taking over at a fast pace, we now have a safer and better alternative that will slowly come to provide a more secure mean of remote connection. And while REST API has not made its way into the core of WordPress yet, you could take precautionary steps and disable the XML-RPC, as it is active by default on WordPress-powered websites, which would yield an immediate improvement to the security and stability of your site.

REST API revenue sources

As REST API is evolving, and is so near the finish line in terms of core integration, new possibilities for creating and receiving monetary incentives are popping up. Overall, WordPress and different plugins and platforms are open source and thus have a big pool of contributors and users who constantly improve and then use them. Most such products are the results of common efforts where thousands of developers and enthusiasts put in their time and then get to make use of a finished tool. This is probably one of the best things about how open-source platforms work, yet even open-source tools cannot always be at the ease of use for all users, and this is how premium products appear. Most of the time these would be the initial product which has had its functionality enhanced, even more improved, and with a very user-friendly interface that almost any non-technical user could apply towards their needs. As this is clear, we will understand that REST API will also be used for some commercial products that we can only predict about. Overall, the incentive to help your fellow users, and get a piece of the cake, raises the motivation to create versatile products.

Now that we are so close to REST API's blooming, we could probably review some of the possible ways in which the API will be used, in a premium manner for which the end user would be charged. Considering that the niche of premium WordPress plugins and themes is pretty saturated and it's hard to come up with original ideas in this regard, considering as a next step the WP REST API could be a very wise business decision.

Mobile applications

Mobile applications will most likely see a huge revamp in regard to REST API and how it will be used for connecting remotely with your website. Given the technical possibilities and the common API for all WordPress sites, generic applications that connect with your site and somehow improve and manage your site from mobile devices are a niche that is believed to have huge potential. As it has been a few years now since we realized that the Web was making a huge move from desktops to mobile devices, we could consider this market to probably be the one where a lot of money will be made. More specifically, because the market is so big, as WordPress powers nearly 25% of all websites on the Web, the users will most likely be interested in having even more control over their websites from mobile devices. Besides the official WordPress application for mobiles, which has enough functionality for what WordPress can offer, there is not much of an alternative, and this is pretty easy to understand as the potential for remote control via the WP REST API and how it connects to your site has not yet been uncovered. The first ones to create applications covering this path will be those who will make the first revolutionary steps, and the majority of the market will be more than likely to make use of this innovative and secure solution.

Wearable devices

I consider wearable devices to be the second niche market after mobile applications to apply the functionality of the REST API and make a market out of this. While wearables have not yet proven to be as dominant as mobile devices, it is still pretty clear that the main functionality these devices provide is fetching data from other applications and websites and displaying it on more convenient smaller screens like those of watches. Because they rely so much on retrieving and receiving data from other sources, REST API will be more than useful for fetching user data from WordPress websites.

SaaS services

SaaS services are very likely to become heavily affected in a positive way when the REST API strikes them. As WordPress is no longer used for blogging purposes only by companies and is more and more tied to their products, the arrival of the API will create new ways for software developers to provide integration of frontend and backend that will definitely yield something that will provide a new foundation for further SaaS applications, given how stable, safe, and (thanks to WP REST API) extensive a solution the REST API is.

Third-party apps

Third-party applications are probably another direction that the REST API will take in regard to its use, given the new possibilities that will allow a more thorough integration of WordPress with third-party applications by big players like Google and Facebook. I believe there is little functionality in WordPress right now in this regard because of the absence of a fully functioning API, which will be soon solved by the REST API. It will be interesting to see how WordPress is able to provide extra functionality to these third-party applications, and the other way around, meaning that the combination of two different platforms with different functionality will result in a totally different product at the outcome, which in the end will mean new possibilities for conducting business and product monetization.

Web services

Web services are a set of technologies, that power the Internet we know today, which are so powerful that their outcomes are the software, programs and services we use today on the Web. Given the flexible environment that the Internet is, and the continuous development it has been undergoing for more than two decades, several solid foundations have been built, which we developed even further in order to bring even broader functionality, better services and platforms to our end users. Most of the standards that the Web has are built on HTTP, and were designed for laying at the foundation of several web platforms and services. Standards that would be compatible with REST are what we will go over, and we will see how they are used in practice to bring the Remote Procedure Call implementation of applications via HTTP. RPC styles might sometimes be appropriate and at times other solutions have to be brought up.

One thing to consider is that our modern services and tools could create web services easily, and thus programming languages such as Java or C# could prove this theory right. If you are using these tools to create RPC-style web services then it is very likely that it won't matter to you, as RESTful services are as simple as they could be. If you are providing services or platforms of the types discussed previously, it is important to understand how valuable these basic web protocols are, and that maintaining the same code structure and standards is pretty valuable, including and not limited to RESTful web services.

REST was not thought of as architecture in its beginnings, and with it currently undergoing transitions and improvements, REST has got to be perceived for what it is as a framework. As the common practices and best way to apply them have not been so clear for REST, a concrete architecture based on REST is needed as a set of guidelines and directions that will show the potential of services fulfilling the Web.

Competing architectures on the Web

As a group of web services, it is important to outline the competition that is happening between three main services, which are RESTful services, the RPC-style ones, and the combination of these two, which are hybrid REST-RPC combinations.

RESTful architectures

Our main concern is the RESTful web service architectures, which is why we will start with an overview of them. Within the architectures of the RESTful systems, information goes straight to the HTTP method, while in resource-oriented architectures, the information goes into the URL. Within the first line of the request sent to HTTP to a resource-oriented RESTful web service lies the info about the desire of the client. The remaining details can be made with one line of code and if the HTTP method does not correspond with the method information, then it is to be considered that the service is not a RESTful one and if the information isn't within the URI, the service will correspondingly not be thought of as a resource-oriented one. To bring up a few examples, most common web services that rely on RESTful, resource-oriented, would be static websites, storing services such as the Amazon S3 one, and read-only websites like Yahoo or Google. As a method of exception we could also say that web services that do not rely on SOAP could be RESTful.

RPC architectures

A web service of the RPC style is an architecture that will receive client data and then send it back, all this while the information is kept within message formats like HTTP and SOAP. The HTTP format is considered to be the most popular one, given how every web service uses it in some way. One thing to note is that web services based on RESTful will share familiar acronyms and names because they are built in a common way and thus have the same interface that they rely on.

As XML-RPC is the most common protocol for web-services and as you can obviously deduct it is based on the RPC architecture, it works as a legacy protocol that will model a programming language in which you would call a function with arguments and then return the value back. As an example, we could say that any service that relies on the HTTP POST value is very likely to be an RPC-style service, and such examples actually tend to move towards combined versions of REST and RPC.

Combination of REST and RPC

One interesting combination to highlight is the REST-RPC architectures (also named **HTTP + POX**), which are in their way a hybrid of not very well developed structures. Given HTTP's way of functioning, an RPC service would use plain HTTP and its URIs would end up being either RESTful ones or combinations, which is something that could cause conflicting structures, or architectures that are not clearly defined, and in the end it would all create confusion.

Overview of architectures

As there are a bunch of technologies relating to the Web, we should probably take a look at web services and the architectures that are at the bottom of each.

HTTP is the most common architecture, as all web services make use of this. If we would send a request towards a web service that is a RESTful one, the method information will be put in the HTTP method and then looked after within the HTTP header, URI or body.

URIs, are strings of characters which are being used with the aim of identifying a resource and then enabling further interaction with the resources of a network by making use of protocols. In RPC architectures, an URI is exposed for every process of handing these procedure calls, while in RESTful services the URI would be exposed for every piece of data that operations will be performed upon.

JavaScript and WordPress

Ever since the rise of REST API, JavaScript has risen in popularity among WordPress users and the WordPress developer circles. In this context, developers have started to enhance their JavaScript skills so they can be ready whenever the REST API strikes, and in the words of Mullenweg, a more JavaScript-oriented WordPress will rise.

JavaScript, being a front-end development language, runs on the client side (the user's device) and can be used for different things such as creating visual interactions on the site (through its jQuery library). In simple words, a library is just a code repository that can be used to enhance the functionality of the fundamental language. Libraries rely on shortcuts and functions to build upon the coding language. This is similar to a framework that also works like a sort of an extension of the initial foundation, yet it wouldn't work like an independent library in an isolated system, it would more be paired with these libraries. Short-codes that are created with templating systems will allow the use of repeating code chunks, thus avoiding the need to write code that has been already written twice.

As there are a bunch of JavaScript libraries, it might be difficult to set a specific one, which is why you should always have an appreciation of the situation and understand what your exact needs are and how you will apply the features of this library or framework within your projects. It is possible to use two libraries at the same time and all of them are free to use and open source.

jQuery is the most common and well-known library belonging to JavaScript. The chance is you might have heard about jQuery many more times than you have heard about JavaScript. WordPress also relies heavily on this library and it is understandable, given the extended functionality for frontend effects that is achieved via jQuery.

AJAX in WordPress

AJAX is a flexible and versatile tool that provides developers the possibility of creating improved applications, and an example of its functionality would be to check credentials upon sending them to the server. Given the asynchronous way in which AJAX works, the entire page doesn't have to be reloaded to receive new data, which is probably why WordPress is so compatible with AJAX and how it interacts with it.

AJAX, in its essence, is a combination of several programming languages, which would be XML and JavaScript. The name Asynchronous JavaScript and XML might or might not be self-explanatory, yet its function is to send data to the server by the means of JavaScript and then return this data in a different, now an XML format.

AJAX, in its manifestation, works to commit small changes or updates for the site visited by the user, without having to send a request for a full page load, meaning that it will be a more efficient way of committing locally rather than a global refresh, which could obviously be more time and resource inefficient and overall not logical given the availability of AJAX.

When talking about AJAX and its pair with WordPress, it is important to note that the former is independent of the latter in the sense that there are no limitations imposed in terms of how it can be implemented. It will be used for applying performance increases to minor changes on the UI, and AJAX comes to play a significant role in applying not necessarily the most significant changes. Given how un-bloated and easy AJAX in itself is, there's no reason to not do some exploration in this direction. It is also worth noting that the official plugin repository of WordPress has a good bunch of available plugins that you could take a look at. One worthwhile thing to say is that given the basic dynamics of AJAX within WordPress, it will yield even more smooth experiences for your users compared to what you could have achieved with HTML for frontend and PHP for backend alone, mainly because it uses WordPress as server-side code and JavaScript on the client side.

While the main function of AJAX is to create a local refresh of webpages, as in not having to have your page refreshed to see updated front-end content, it is thus an easy way to fetch data from a WordPress site and then use it in your frontend code, and it is the best solution to take a more creative approach to the issue as in seeking for what interesting results can possibly come up. A parallel for this would be REST API and how creatively we actually could and do use it, way beyond its technical on-paper functionality.

Things to consider when using REST API

Whenever in the close future REST API lands in the core of WordPress, lots of innovative movements will be made in this regard, including the solution of a bunch of issues that have been around for quite a while and, given the technical limitations, we couldn't see anything but temporary fixes or methods of bypassing them that were not very reliable. While the WordPress REST API will bring many great things to WordPress as a CMS and as a platform as a whole, it is to be understood that it is no magic pill that will put WordPress on steroids and totally revamp the way we feel, build and present the Web overnight. While I believe the transition over to REST will be achieved fairly easy and quickly, it is no secret that it will still have issues and irregularities, moreover there will be times when you probably wouldn't want to make use of REST API, even if you technically could. It's a known psychological fact that once something is uncovered and revealed after a long period of expectation and waiting, its use can easily go beyond its boundaries and even if REST API becomes an established API, there will be situations in which you could and should ignore its use.

The main point of REST API is hooking APIs provided by third-party platforms with WordPress and then providing the functionality of either of those and improving its functionality. Given that WordPress is based on PHP you could also take advantage of this by making it the ground foundation for your application, and only using the REST API to connect with this foundation. Examples of this use would be applications built in JavaScript that in their turn would have complex data use, and all this without using anything but WordPress, JavaScript and the REST API for interlinking.

Interacting with databases using REST API

REST API would be useful for mobile applications as well, in the way that they grab the data on your website and deliver it on these mobile devices, which could be something more than just some **read-only** kind of content and could literally recreate the **desktop** experience on those devices. Provided that you are familiar with the basics of APIs, you know that they already provide a one-way functionality in the way they receive information from the source and then display it, but this is the basic kind of interaction we have had since the beginning of APIs and is not much changed in this regard. With the REST API, however, we will be creating real interactions at a whole other level, the API level, where we could actually transfer and receive data both ways, meaning that you will no longer have only the **reading** of data from one way, but something more complicated and interesting.

The interesting part comes when completely static websites built in other languages, but using PHP for the backend, start linking to WordPress in order to fetch data from that site. This is good if your initial aim was to avoid building your site on PHP and then interlinking it to one by means of REST API.

The use of WordPress REST API in applications is an entire topic of discussion with various opinions about which cases you would need to use it for, and in which cases it is better avoided. I will try to shorten this up to the most important topics of the discussion. The most important thing to note is that REST API is meant to provide extensive functionality that some basic solutions cannot provide. In this case, if you have a simple website, simple application and everything is functional for you, it is very likely that you will not need the REST API in one way or another. An interesting way to put it would be to think about whether you ever missed anything relating to your site or application before hearing about REST API. The API could be really useful for creating similar experiences to apps, and in cases where you want to avoid building and working with PHP, except where you are linking to a PHP-based website via the REST API. Most common examples of REST API for possible use in applications would be e-commerce apps, which is something that most online stores are concerned with right now. Mobile e-commerce is rising, the market is huge for providing improved solutions, and thus something like the use of REST API within e-commerce mobile applications will be very much used and welcome, given the possibilities of better experiences that could be built for the mobile end-users.

Doing more with REST API

Another way of working with the REST API would be the default admin screen within WordPress. Again, think about how extensive your needs for customization and change are, because if you are just changing minor things or adding a hook or two, then it is very likely you won't need the REST API and some online tutorials that will teach you how to do modifications in this regard will cut it. A full revamp would, however, not be so possible given the logical restrictions imposed. App-like dashboards and admin interfaces will be possible to be built whenever the REST API hits the core of WordPress.

To be taken into the scope are single page applications that you might have not heard of yet. Given how extensively JavaScript will be used within WordPress, we will no longer have different pages that will be interlinked and will rather have a one-page application that will update, refresh and load content by means of JavaScript. You might already be familiar with such changes on a smaller scale, which were manifested in the admin page of WordPress where certain changes could be made without the page having to refresh. This is pretty innovative and will be thoroughly exploited, in a positive way, given how efficient, easy and fast such websites will be. Such applications will be fun and user-friendly, but the benefits of these services will end here, given that it is not possible for search engines to properly index their content, and thus we can think of it as a coin with two sides. As technology evolves, either websites or search engines will commit towards a change for a friendly pairing, yet that is not the case right now and we may not be sure about what the future holds for us, so at the time of writing, the biggest downside of such applications is the lack of proper indexing by search aggregators.

One thing that I would like to cover, which has only been briefly mentioned before, is the level of development of REST API, which will not be in its perfect state right from the beginning. While there is a solid team of developers working on ever improving the REST API, it is still a means of architecture, plugin, service, solution: no matter the name, it will still be imperfect and have its ups and downs. The solutions that will be brought by the WP REST API will be big, and it's never an easy task covering such things. You could start by experimenting now with the beta v2 version of the plugin, yet you should be careful with using that for anything beside testing purposes, as a real project might be ruined by the unsustainability of the plugin, which is even admitted by the developers themselves. Overall, WordPress as a CMS has been thoroughly examined, its biggest drawbacks and pros are known, major security vulnerabilities have been addressed, and the huge pool of plugins and themes available on the market can easily allow thorough customization if that is what you are looking for. Not only will using the REST API in its first versions of the release be tiresome and time-consuming, it might well raise unknown issues that will only be fixed in upcoming versions.

There have been thoughts that the REST API will be a very good fit for enterprise solutions and thus provide extensive functionality even for the big players, and while it can be hard to disagree with this opinion, given how well we speak of the said API, I am pretty sure websites and applications at such a scale will avoid its use in the first phases of official release, precisely because of the reasons mentioned previously.

It is important to recall Matt Mullenweg's words about how JavaScript will play a big role in WordPress' future development phases, and thus developers who are highly proficient in both CMS and JavaScript will probably be the ones to bring the first examples of how far we can take the REST API. Overall, it is just important to properly understand how extensive your requirements and desires are in regard to your application or software, and decide whether you actually need the functionality of REST API or you whether you don't, and if you could just make use of the REST API from the beginning while other alternatives address your needs, then I would reconsider this position, at least while the initial possible bugs and irregularities are cleared.

Current status of REST API

The biggest yearly event about WordPress has recently taken place, the WordCamp US, which was held in Philadelphia. Nearly 2000 WordPress enthusiasts, developers and fans attended the event and quite a few ideas were noted there. First of all, Matt Mullenweg, the founder of WordPress, said that up to 25% of the Web is powered by the CMS he founded, and amongst other interesting stats, REST API was given some attention as well. He stated that the opportunities that the WP REST API is bringing for the CMS, applications powered by JavaScript, and third-party apps is immense given the innovation level that will be brought. Calypso, the new architectural foundation for WordPress.com has not been left without a notice, but we will cover that example a little later. Matt said that developers have actually learned JavaScript in order to approach even more to the current state of WordPress, and that he strongly believes that JavaScript and API-driven interfaces represent the future of the Web and WordPress included. He also considers that backwards compatibility (which in the latest version of the REST API is not that good) can be left behind in cases like ours where progress is at stake.

While the emphasis on JavaScript and APIs has been big, it is believed that PHP will not go away just yet, and that the success of WordPress is the foundation it has been built upon, which is PHP. It might be the case for now, but the transition to JavaScript is fast and consistent, so the thought that the importance of PHP will only continue to diminish becomes more and more realistic.

The weakness of WordPress is the lack of extensive customization, in the words of Matt Mullenweg. His encouragement for his fellow contributors was to consider learning

JavaScript and building JavaScript-powered interfaces specifically. He thinks it will represent not only the future of WordPress but also the future of the Web and that developers should consider taking such a direction. He also emphasized the freedom of the Web and how important it is to keep improving open-source platforms and openness on the Web, and that we could make use of the API-driven development to make progress in this direction.

WordPress features

Now, moving from the creator of WordPress to the team behind WP REST API, who say there are a few issues about the API, and in specific the **post**, **term**, **user** and **comment** endpoints. These items cover autosaves, post previews, password-protected posts and meta handling that the team looks to tackle via a feature plugin rather than holding back from getting the API to merge. Ryan McCue, who is the project lead, said that these concerns will not be supported as of yet and will be covered in a separate plugin that will come to be as an additional enhancement to the API in future, so that the API isn't limited in its development by this drawback.

Ryan also said that the core objects of read, create, update and delete would be merged in the core as of now, with other features to come and they will be implemented when they are ready. This doesn't make Matt Mullenweg very comfortable, as he considers a partial API is not the best thing to be integrated within the core of WordPress, while in his turn McCue stated that the API should be perceived as an ever-enhancing service rather than an unfinished one. His point is that flexibility and a structure permitting progressive growth would be the key difference in the current APIs.

In regard to how we could use the REST API for customization, we have stated that admin page modifications would be one of the key features, and it is a bit surprising to state that while the four core object types will provide some room for innovation in themes and content editors, full replacements relating to `wp-admin` are not really possible at this stage. While the hype is big around REST API, including a conference dedicated solely to it, most of the developers who really build things with the REST API would be the contributors and Matt Mullenweg has seconded this opinion, stating that while he does have huge interest in it, considering it to be the most promising thing out there at this moment, his skepticism can be understood given that he considers that there's not even XML-RPC pairing in regard to features from the API. He also said that REST API somehow resembles doing something that could already be done before. It all ends up with contributors disagreeing with Matt Mullenweg over whether the WP REST API is an incomplete API or not, and that there would be too many drawbacks in the current API for it to be included in the core right away. The development of the plugin in this regard is slow, and it has insufficient testing for it to become a core part.

REST API conclusion

The conclusion stated that Matt Mullenweg will probably not go ahead with a plugin with partial endpoints in the core, and that for the REST API to make a move towards the core a complete API must be built, given the millions of sites that will be affected, whether positively or negatively. As a personal take on it, I would say that both parties do have consistent arguments and it is to be understood why both of them are advocating for the reasons that were brought up.

The main concern at this point is whether the endpoints are ready enough, and thus whether the main purpose of the API has been fulfilled or not. It is the incomplete support of the `wp-admin` features that brings up issues and limits the future movement of REST API, for now. The proposal for solving this was to take a step towards progressive enhancement, as that is the key solution to the related problems that would unblock the REST API project and work done on it so far, and still provide a solid amount of support for handling data types within WordPress. The discussion still continues amongst contributors on the topic of iterative development within the core of WordPress, or the delivery of an improved and complete API. Given that fact, adoption is surrounding the project because of the dependency of the API on a plugin. It all comes down to whether the contributors will agree with the opinion of Matt Mullenweg, that the plugin has to be polished and improved, or whether they insist on inclusion of the endpoints against his recommendations.

At the moment, it is clear that the REST API will make it towards the core at some point in the near future, yet a firm date still cannot be set given the inconsistencies of the API that Matt Mullenweg is concerned about.

Progressive enhancement of WP REST API

With the established progress within the REST API community, there is one perspective that definitely deserves more attention and consideration, which is why we talk about the progressive enhancement of the WordPress REST API, which is the development route proposed by the contributor team behind the API for its future. With the imperfection that Matt Mullenweg considers to be the problem holding up the REST API's integration in the core, progressive enhancement comes as a proposed solution for forward-compatibility with upcoming releases of WordPress and the way robust handling of data types is handled in WordPress. It is said that progressive enhancement would unblock the REST API from its state, as parity with every feature of the WordPress is admittedly considered to be the wrong approach, says McCue.

Custom Post types have that freedom in regard to working with data and a robust system that indicates feature support via the REST API. For example, post types that don't have the editor support flag won't have their **content** registered, just as the admin will not show the content editor to the aforementioned post types.

Progressive enhancement would also provide feature detection for future versions of WordPress, so clients have a reliable paradigm to see if WordPress will support a certain feature before putting it to use. The progressive enhancement that already exists within the REST API is easily accessible by clients that would like to have robustness. McCue argues the necessity for `autosave` support and post previews, which are not yet built in, by arguing that WordPress admin already does this through `localStorage` for offline connections, for which server-side support is not required.

A feature that will not be present for the time being in the API will still be worked on and added in upcoming major WordPress releases, with a corresponding mark for feature availability as mentioned above. Given the way REST API endpoints are registered with two parts to their name, the route and the namespace, plugins that are available on the site could also be detected.

As a final thought on the current state of REST API and WordPress, the contributors to the API are sure that WordPress needs to move forward and they are being limited in delivering a sustainable solution because of the absence of core integration. They say that in their consideration the correct approach would be to continue the API development, and that progressive enhancement is a paradigm that the project has got to adopt if it ever wants to see the light of day in regard to progress.

WordPress Calypso and the REST API

While the mentioned lack of clarity regarding how REST API evolves as project for the time being, there's also been an important event for WordPress last year, which was the release of Calypso—the so-called new WordPress.com, which is a single interface that will let you manage all your WordPress.com or JetPack websites. That interface will definitely bring improvements to everyone who has their websites hosted on the previously-limited WordPress.com platform. Calypso works as an entirely new application that will create interactions with your site by using REST API, and will be available to everyone with a website hosted at the .com version of the CMS or anyone who has the Jetpack plugin installed.

Calypso will pretty much let you do anything in regard to your content and some minor site edits and changes, with the exception of customizing your theme, but the limitation is not that great given the innovation in remove control and speed that has been brought by the means of Calypso. It probably also represents the potential and influence that the REST API will have upon WordPress overall, and Calypso is just a small example of what heights can be reached by the means of REST API.

Securing a REST API

In order to cover the best ways of securing the REST API, it would be a good idea to start with the standard authentication protocols that make it easy to secure that API. As a general rule it's always better to stick to these common protocols, as custom protocols should only be used in certain situations.

The first protocol to be mentioned is basic authentication with TLS, which is the easiest one to implement given that it requires no additional libraries for proper use as the standard framework contains everything that is needed. The low security level compared to other protocols that this method of authentication offers is probably the biggest drawback, with no advanced options available for using this protocol as only the username and password are encoded in Base64. It is also a requirement to use this method of authentication over a secure connection or TLS encryption, given that the credentials could be easily decoded.

OAuth protocol

OAuth 2.0, which is the next version of the OAuth protocol, focuses on simplicity while providing specific methods of authorization for applications, mobile phones and other devices. This is a secure and tested signature-based protocol that will make a cryptographic signature combined with secret token, nonce and other request information.

Another technique to make use of would be the generated API keys, which instead of traditional credentials, use longer series of random characters that are not so easy to randomly guess. These credentials are typically smaller in length and will make use of common words that would generally be more insecure than subjects of brute force and dictionary attacks. Passwords should be avoided when possible because with every password change your API will fail.

In best practice it is stated that passwords have to be encrypted within the database to limit a possible data breach, which would increase the overhead whenever a user sends an authentication request. Avoiding sessions for the REST API has also proven to be a good practice for improving the API server performance.

WordPress API and regular users

The main overviews of the REST API that we have looked at only concerned the contributors and developer's side and how REST will improve their lives. We have stated countless times how important the REST API is for the entire community, yet we haven't gone into much detail about how these end users will specifically profit out of it. The idea of REST API making the WordPress CMS move from being a content management system towards becoming an application platform is heard very often, but it has some good reasoning behind it. While the conversation on the topic of REST API is pretty loud, we shall see how a simple end user is involved and even if they cares about how the REST API is moving forward. It has been suggested that developers learn JavaScript, but what about the regular Joe?

It is worth noting whether, even if there is so much hype about WordPress relying more on JavaScript and it becoming an application rather than a CMS, it might concern the ultimate user who is interested in some regular blogging. At its beginning, WordPress was also only a blogging system that users made use of, yet at one stage the blogging system turned into a whole new content management one, and that has not influenced those who were interested just in blogging. Furthermore, they were actually provided with even better blogging experiences, given the features a content management system has brought.

REST API moving WordPress from a CMS to an application platform will most likely not impact you in any way if you're just a regular user who has no intention of using extensive functionality. The main areas of development in this regard would be the admin management screens and the JavaScript themes.

The very best example of how end users profit from the REST API would be the Calypso desktop application, which actually showed how extensive modification changed the default preview screens. The drastic improvement in content editing and interfaces has improved the overall experience for all WordPress.com users, including for others who have their websites on the self-hosted version of the CMS, as long as they have the Jetpack plugin installed. In future versions of Calypso, it is probable that it will become independent from Jetpack, and will provide even more extensive and versatile functionality, including a merge between the REST API of WordPress.com and the self-hosted version.

Other examples of this could be more bespoke admin systems that will emerge and could eventually be run on desktops and mobile screens. Development of such admin screens could and most likely will go beyond just the WordPress interfaces, given the fact that other site management possibilities like the one within the hosting industry could be established.

Another direction that REST API could take to benefit the end users could be WordPress expendables such as plugins and themes, which will use the REST API in pair with JavaScript to provide single page application type sites. Given that every interaction will be based on JavaScript alone, a lot of more extensive stuff could be built. This would cover calendars, invoicing systems and budget management applications. Overall, this kind of service and application would be time consuming and costly to build, especially in the beginning phases of the REST API when not every developer will have the thorough expertise to build such applications, and when not all bugs and issues will have been addressed. Another thing to highlight would be the hype that is covering the surroundings of REST API so well, such that huge progress will be made towards it and far less will be focused on other services, APIs, development in other potential directions and eventually supporting the current users that the CMS has. While it is to be understood that over the past 13 years WordPress has grown well enough to not be some inflexible platform, and it will obviously not be forgotten whichever API pops up on the scene, yet the REST API is just one of the concerns and not the concern, no matter how much discussion is going on around it.

Building your own API

When talking about APIs and building them, it is important to understand that the process might be a little bit difficult at first if you're not acquainted with the patterns and best practices that lie at the foundation of each API, yet the process is not as complicated as it might seem at first glance. It is to be set that every API must connect to a server and then return some kind of data, for which a corresponding code to back it up will be necessary. Potential requirements could also include authentication and rate limiting. The endpoints are the fundamental architecture that lies at the bottom of an API, which are responsible for returning things with specific attributes. Making it as simple as possible is the key here. The return type data is another consideration that has to be taken care of. The majority of web users would expect some JSON content, and the alternative for this would be XML. The Web developers however, have established JSON as the fundamental API return type, so you are probably better off sticking with it for now.

When beginning with the development of the rather simple REST API, you would start by using the REST packages and then defining the API, getting it to run a web framework, creating the documentation and finally running the API in client libraries. The foundation of a REST API is a resource that is defined by using one of the **resource** types from the `rest-core`, it being the data type that will represent a singular resource. It is usually made of two parameters, and specifically the context you would be getting from the parent resource and the context that will be received upon resource identification. It can also be used for sending data to other sub-resources that will have type parameters as their identifiers for the resource. Upon defining the resource, you would have to cover other kinds of handlers if there are more fields that are defining handlers for your resource. Moving forward, you will have to work with more complicated identifiers and then take care of error handling within the handlers. Once that resource has been defined completely, you would combine it with others within the API and that will happen by composing resources within the API. You will then provide a version that will be assigned to your API, which will then be run and generate documentation along client code.

There have also been various spin-offs from building a normal API, and one would be the creation of a REST API for a mobile application using Node.js, and how it will connect to iOS and Android. Node.js has proven to be a reliable way of building mobile APIs and the reasons for that are the ease of working with JSON in JavaScript, the light weight of the Node.js library, and the control that is permitted over requests and responses. Handling authentication is a big thing whenever building an API. Authentication would refer to the practice of understanding who exactly accessed your data and securing this entire connect. You would usually only need a runtime for your application, which would be the Node.js, some framework for building the Node.js applications, an HTTP client that will permit the making of custom requests to the REST API, and to finish off, some backend service that will handle user authentication.

Drawbacks of a custom API

A downside of building your own custom API is the fact that figuring out a perfect API strategy that will be really functional is hard at times, and here we will try and see what the disadvantages of building your own REST API would be. RESTful approaches in development are pretty hard given the fact that a client-side and server-side interaction is required and that a single set of requirements is required for both sides, including testing and actually building the client-side and server-side parts. There's also the fact that given the plentitude of available, modern technologies, it's pretty tiresome to create an ideal development cycle and process. Interface negotiation would have to happen between both parties, and that consumes efforts from both sides, which makes it harder to see the project finish line, yielding a lack of satisfaction for all parties.

Money and time consumption is not the only hassle that is very expensive and time consuming, there is also the fact that the application has to run seamlessly and as designed. A common case is when a project is moving forward but new requirements pop up that were not anticipated, in which case going back and expanding the boundaries of the old REST services is not possible because they will already be in development, in which case new REST API services have to be created for every new project.

Depending on the size of the project, it might be a real-life situation in which the process of building the API takes quite extended amounts of time, which also includes different mechanisms for security, credential strategies and systems for management that in the end will result in chaos or at least some inconsistent clutter.

This example mostly concerns businesses and similar enterprise projects covering REST APIs, where there are big production teams working on one project or platform, yet this is still an issue that has to be addressed somehow. It is probably a better idea to start by identifying the data sources that would be accessed by the applications and then creating a reusable REST API platform that will be able to support general purpose application development.

Within some projects, there has been an attempt to address complex problems by making use of API Management software pieces, which would allow existing REST APIs to be linked with a proxy server which in turn would expose the APIs in a unified way, including extra features like usage reporting and throttling of the API.

REST API management

One big problem is that companies do not rely on creating a unified API that would be somewhat fundamentally generalist to be used for future applications and web services, which is why it's necessary to have such a unified proxy for API management.

One more way of taking care of the complex data security issue is to implement the Mobile Device Management, which will ignore the server-side mess and will control data access straight from the client side, yet because more flexible solutions are expected to be delivered, this particular one is not so good as it is harder to maintain.

In order solve the complexity that has been discussed, control access to the data should be prioritized over the device, as this would permit developers to build any kind of client applications that they might want with an existing architecture. This would represent a step forward for efficiency, because it would unlink the server-side development from the client-side one in a manner that would positively affect the speed and thus the development cycle.

Backend compatibility issues raise scalability, security and efficiency issues that would then create powerful REST API creation tools as the API Management and Mobile Device Management do not solve the root of the issue. They can only be considered as temporary solutions, which would cover up for the inconsistencies for a while, yet in the long-term this only causes drawbacks.

It would be worthwhile taking a moment to talk about the advantages that reusable web services have in terms of application development. It is actually possible to create a reusable REST API platform in the first place, even if the most common practice is to create new services for each individual project. Reusable interfaces have got to be flexible by design and that would be manifested via their filter string parameters, which would allow for dynamic querying of any SQL database. The service would then provide support for arrays of objects and anything related, which is returned in the same transaction. This would support a large number of patterns, which will not need any customization. These services will then cover several scenarios for which they are used, for example considering SQL interfaces we would be in need of support for data pagination, array sorting, record-level access control and so on. There could also be ANSI corner cases, where the date and time formats need to be handled consistently across various types of SQL databases.

Implementation of custom services for REST API

There are also special cases that have to be taken care of in a special way, for example a server-side scripting engine will have the responses and requests changed for it to handle workflow triggers, field validation, custom usage limitations and so on. The engine used for scripting can be used for implementation of custom services whenever this is necessary and access to an external web service will be just another way of improving the functionality that a reusable REST API service platform would have.

Whatever your aim is, it is important for a company to set a strategy that relies on reusable interfaces, as this would be logical. This would only create consistency, eliminate clutter and create a logical flow for further development. Unlinking development from the two client-side and server-side phases would only provide room for improvement as the safety of such applications would increase as well. Because client-side `devs` will have the possibility of making use of the identical REST API for the same project, they will have a broader mean of data access, which would power their applications. Data objects or parameters could be all different, but the fact that the programming style would remain the same is clear, and this will yield in an improved API that will be able to minimize the differences between SQL, NOSQL and file storage. It is pretty hard not to agree that such a level of consistency of services would only provide an easier way of learning the API and thus writing applications, which could also benefit from the virtualization provided by the service layer if they were written on a service platform. As services wouldn't be tied to a specific piece of the backend infrastructure, the service could be installed anywhere, and thus the movement of the application among places of storage could be easily performed.

Overall, the advantages would come to provide profound improvements for client-side developers, server-side admins and anyone who will end up using this application, given the improved structure, clean formatting and solid foundation.

Integration of REST API with mobile applications

One last approach to be noted here is the integration of REST API and mobile applications, which has been covered in the points above. Here, I would like to outline a few more specific details, which relate to the insufficiency of functionality that a REST API will provide whenever integrating with a mobile app.

A complete solution representing a backend foundation for mobile or web applications would face a few issues that have to be addressed. Every API has got to be backed up by documentation if client developers want to understand how to make good use of the service, and for that there would be several URLs for every application that is developed and tested. Given the fact that every URL will have identifiers for various types of resources, URL parameters might be required in order to take various arguments. Each service will then have HTTP verbs that will set the permitted operations over the resource, with a common return of JSON documents. Client developers need to grasp the formatting of these requests and responses, which would be difficult to solve because the format is different, being based on various parameters.

Custom platforms for the REST API are often administered with command-line operations and server logs. Configuring services, uploading applications and managing permissions might sometime require considerable tech knowledge and thus it is a better solution to provide an administrative console that in turn would not have such great requirements for technical knowledge to successfully change the backend platform. This would also create the possibility for improved development, as in the absence of requiring master database credentials that would then be used by other developers. While this does sound like a correct solution, it is a tedious task to create an admin console of such a level that all its capabilities are available as RESTful services as well. The way to go in this situation would be to prepare a set of services for the backend developers that would then build this administration console on the ready platform, which in its turn would need extra services for administration.

Standards for custom REST APIs

If you were to build a REST API alone it wouldn't be the hardest task ever, but if you are not doing this for personal skill development or just as a small work project, and it is a major project instead, then extensive functionality might be required for the application. Portability might be one of these requirements, and in that case you would have to switch from an app towards other places of storage. A specific trait of REST APIs that have been custom built is that they have hard-wired connections to different databases and pieces of backend infrastructure, which again makes it more difficult. In an ideal environment, the backend of your REST API would be installed on any place of storage, which would provide portability during all phases of development and flexibility for all those involved in the production, testing and eventually development of this application.

Custom REST APIs have a few issues that almost always surround them, and those are concerns about reliability, security and flexibility/scalability. It is important that any piece of software or web service follows the highest standards and only proceeds to apply the best measures in regard to the three directions, yet there a few things to be outlined that I would like to mention. The fact that the foundation has got to be really solid is without question and thus checks against SQL attacks, record-level access control and management of credentials, the process of sign-up and routing engine exploits have to be performed. System reliability seems to be very important for transactional hosting and thus the requirement for limits to be put on service transactions, which in turn cover the usage of a particular client. Server outages and requests that take too long to be performed would be another headache you would need to be aware of, and so you should actually realize how much is needed in order for a scalable and more importantly secure RESTful service to see the light of day. Overall, it is important to understand that building your own REST API might result in a big clutter with eventual issues for your backend if you do not have the proper expertise to tackle such issues in your projects. Another idea is that reusable REST API services, which are proven to be the most efficient and reliable, would require time and effort to be carefully crafted and built. Besides, the REST API is just a small part of the entire system, and even if you get to develop a good API, it doesn't really mean that you managed to create a secure RESTful foundation.

Custom API tokens

Authentication based on tokens has been around for quite a while and rightfully, given the common use of APIs, tokens have proved to be one of the best ways of handling authentication for a bunch of users. While there are other means of authentication, the main features that this authentication provides are that it is mobile-application ready, and has improved security and extensive scalability which when it works as implied is more than enough for smooth authentication. Any significant web application that you might have used, like any social media hub, makes use of token-based authentication and we will go through the reasons why they took that path. Given that the protocol of HTT (HTTP) is stateless, the authentication of a user just with his credentials will not produce any result, as these details wouldn't have anything to be paired with to confirm the authentication, which is why user information is stored server-wide and is used whenever somebody makes a request for a session or a log-in within the system is attempted. Scalability is, however, not the strong suit of this method, which is why we have slowly started to swim away from this method. This method worked fine up to the point where there were no better alternatives, yet the fact that such a method was hard on the speed and performance respectively, had limited scalability and it was impossible to expand the data across several mobile devices means it is no longer usable for us.

Differently to storing information on the server during a session, token-based authentication is stateless and thus will not store any kind of information about a user on the server during any session. Scalability is thus possible, given that no information is stored during a session. Upon the request for access that is sent by means of credentials, the application then validates these credentials and will further provide a signed token to the client, who will store the provided token and send it along with every request relating to him, which in the end will be checked by the server, which will respond with data. The HTTP header will be responsible for holding the token with every request. After authentication has been successfully completed, we could perform a multitude of things with this token and even create permission-based tokens that could be paired with third-party applications, which in turn would pass along the data granted by means of a concrete token.

As for the benefits of tokens, their stateless state and scalability would be the first ones to mark and note, as their load balancers can pass a user along to any server given that there is no state or session information placed anywhere. Keeping information on a user that is logged in could generate wrong traffic spikes for the same users, who would be repeatedly sent to the same server that received their information upon log-in. As the token itself works as an information holder, such issues no longer arise. As every request would have a token sent as well and no cookie is sent along it, CSRF attacks are prevented and even in case of specific implementation the token is stored within a cookie on the client side and thus there is no information that could be manipulated. As tokens are meant to expire after a set unit of time, a request to log in again might happen. There's a term of token revocation that would allow the setting of certain tokens as invalid.

With regard to future development possibilities, the means of authentication with tokens open, it should be stated that applications that share permissions with each other will continue to expand and yield curious results. Tokens are the right solution for providing selective permissions to third-party applications, and we could even hand out permission tokens that our users wanted to provide access data.

Multiple platforms and domains would also be a concern if you were looking broadly in terms of development of your applications and how many users would authenticate through it. In this regard, access to several devices and applications has got to be provided so as not to impose flexibility limits on end users. As the API will just be used to serve data, making asset serving from a content delivery network would actually get rid of the issues that CORS brings up, which we have mentioned earlier, so our data will be available for access to anyone who is known to have a valid token for the purpose.

As a conclusion on how authentication tokens work, I would like to say that while token authentication does have a few drawbacks, that is not our concern right now as the drawbacks definitely do not overcome the positive parts that the token authentication brings. Overall, the way tokens store credential data within them and the way we can decline certain tokens is more than a solid solution, and its common use on the Web by big services confirms this once more.

Summary

We have now covered REST API in theory and practice at length. Earlier chapters had taught you a good deal about WordPress REST API and coding. You learnt how to build and manage posts, metadata, apps and a lot more.

This chapter gave you a basic crash course in REST API and its history as well as its future. Of course, for a pure developer, this might not be absolute mandatory to know. But if you wish to know all that there is to know about REST API, this chapter provided useful reading.

We shall now cover the remnants of WP REST API in the final chapter.

9
Summing It Up

In the previous chapter, we discussed in detail the theoretical aspects and origins, as well as the usage and disabling of REST API.

In this final chapter of the book, we will talk about REST API vis a vis XML-RPC, and cover some other theoretical and knowledge-worthy aspects of the same.

Comparison of REST API with XML-RPC

REST represents an architectural style that will set some constraints on interfaces to achieve the desired goal. By using REST, we will enforce a server model where the client wants to gain information and act on some data that would be managed by the server. The very same server then sends a message to the client about the provided resources by a communication between client and server that has got to be cacheable and stateless. All implementations of a REST architectural project are supposed to be RESTful.

RPC, which is defined as the **Remote Procedure Call**, is a mechanism that will provide you with the possibility of calling a procedure in another process and will exchange data by passing some messages. It will process data on the server-side and is sometimes used as one kind of an underlying protocol for message passing which is nothing like HTTP.

RPC versus REST

When comparing RPC and REST architectural styles, it is not that wise from a technical point of view to compare these two methods, as these services work in a form of pairing, rather than comparison between them. On top of any RPC implementation, the RESTful service can be built upon by using methods that will conform to the constraints of REST. HTTP styles REST implementation on the top of an RPC implementation by creating methods for GET, POST, PUT, and DELETE that take in metadata that will mirror some HTTP headers and return a string that will reflect the exact HTTP request. As was admitted, REST is a set of constraints that does not include aspects of the HTTP-specific implementation, and this proves that our service could implement a RESTful interface that would expose methods which are different to the ones that HTTP presents and would still be RESTful.

It has to be admitted that RESTful interfaces can be built using XML-RPC, but there are several reasons that will convince you that doing this is not the best idea, and why you would actually want to make your RPC interface by making good use of XML-RPC techniques, and those reasons would be:

- Caching, versioning, and throttling have existing implementations and can be utilized straight away
- Actions are server-controlled instead of being hard coded within the client by using procedure calls, thus simplifying development
- If you make use of custom procedures , that will result in building narrow RPC interfaces

You might ask yourself why would we even consider using XML-RPC when REST is available to us, and why would we even keep it as an option? It has to be admitted that there's more hassle in writing a client library for XML-RPC, yet every library is more than likely to work with any similar service you would have to deal with, most users never having to write one. As a counter idea, writing a REST client library is easier and has the interpretation that almost everyone has a different idea of what REST is. A separate client module is necessary for every service you use, and REST is of no help with this task. Some interpretations of how REST is implemented do not even closely resemble general ideas about how it is usually applied, which proves that while REST is a way easier solution, it is not necessarily the right method or solution for a particular case.

Advantages of applying REST can be deduced from the points we have discussed above, but nonetheless, we will go through them as well. Overall, it is considered that REST is a way lighter solution compared to XML-RPC, and that supposes that is a better solution when having to work with large datasets. The lightness of REST is especially noticeable when working with JSON. XML-RPC client must load complete responses into the memory, thus it can be displayed as a return value whereas the REST client find it easier to process the stream as it arrives. XML-RPC is going to limit the size of the response (and that is considered to be a norm) while the REST call will respond with any number of records. The XML-RPC will ignore HTTP semantics, being HTTP POSTs. It will benefit from the caching infrastructure where all calls have got to be processed by the target server, enabling the client to check for updates by making use of an HTTP request.

XML-RPC API will make use of the XML format to transfer the data. Being a commonly used markup language and interchanging format, it will most likely support almost all programming languages within standard libraries. The API of XML-RPC within WordPress will pass user credentials as a part of every request, meaning that users will have to provide the application with their account password, which in this instance is not encrypted, meaning that XML-RPC is only totally secure when used over a secure connection (HTTPS) where network users cannot gather sensitive data.

The JSON API, on the other site, will make use of the JSON format for data transfer, which, in its substance, is a lightweight format for object serialization that is going to be limited in syntax yet easy to use with most programming languages. It's very easy to pair it with JavaScript, it being a derivation of its syntax, making it easy to attract the interactive web applications. The JSON API plugin will support mechanisms that are going to allow multiple authentications, including basic HTTP and OAuth 1.0a.

Keypoints

In comparing those two, it is said that REST is an HTTP-based protocol while XML-RPC is XML based, which represents the fundamental difference that displays the further roots that each one has during its processing. REST being an HTTP-based protocol, it will work best when the client represents a browser, yet XML-RPC, being XML based, will make no assumptions regarding the client that uses the protocol, meaning that it will take more effort to process it compared to REST. Each object has its URL and can easily be copied and bookmarked and then cached. The main advantage of XML-RPC is the fact that it is a client independent, and will easily integrate with any application, a capability that does not precisely correspond to REST.

In conclusion, it is important to say that every service provides a solution depending on the problem that is set, the best APIs being considered those that will display a balance of REST and RPC semantics, where the usage would be regarded as most appropriate.

Interacting with third-party services using XML-RPC basic authentication versus interacting with REST API advanced authentication tokens.

Disadvantages of XML-RPC

We will start our comparison with the main disadvantages that are common in the XML-RPC system. The first disadvantage that we will look at is the fact that the subvert intent of XML schema will be considered valid, no matter what the omissions or mistakes on an application-level field. The second con of XML-RPC is the fact that it requires as much as four times the estimated server bandwidth.

The broad availability of libraries that create automatic language-level objects, with the libraries in turn being provided with an advantage over plain XML counterparts, is what stands behind the success of XML-RPC. A more detailed overview of **XmlRPC** disadvantages would be the following:

- Several XML-RPC implementations will fail at producing language-level objects and will instead require a run-time lookup of the fields or other syntaxes
- The open XML support falls short and does not require integration with extensive third-party libraries, and is expected instead to make use of automatically created objects to the application's objects
- The XML-RPC system in itself is *bloated* and not very flexible
- The ability to check the application-level schema is lost if the definition document is used for validating the RPC calls, which sets an unstandardized method for validation protocol
- The deployed HTTP proxies will not be leveraged, and no links from web pages or e-mails will be available
- There is no proper access to it from any browser

As a conclusion to the usage of XML-RPC, it is a fact that it will not provide a solution to every problem, but will instead serve as an effective solution if your only requirement is requesting and receiving information. It will be using XML to encode and decode the remote procedure call, which will be used along with its parameter.

XML-RPC usage in WordPress

WordPress, in itself, is a flexible platform for blogging that is highly customizable and very efficient for pairing with other systems and APIs. The XML-RPC system within WordPress will be the topic of our discussion in this section. XML-RPC within WordPress will help this by performing operations on the installation of WordPress, even remotely, which makes the use of XML-RPC within WordPress natural for pairing with some software that does batch tasking such as creating several posts from a single file.

If we were to take a look at the official WordPress Codex, then we would find that WordPress, being based on an XML-RPC interface, has its implementation for its specific functionality that is called in the WP API. This is suggested for use when possible, as your client should use the API variants that start with the `wp` prefix. It also supports other different APIs. Given the WordPress XML-RPC support, you can post your WordPress blog to several popular weblog clients and go further by expanding with WordPress plugins that modify its behavior. The good thing is that the functionality of XML-RPC has been turned on by default for a long time-**WordPress version 3.5**.

Usage of XML RPC

The XML-RPC system within WordPress is the API, which provides developers who make applications for desktops and mobile devices with the possibility of making a connection with the application and the WordPress-powered site. The beauty of XML-RPC API is that it will provide the developers with a way to write applications that will permit several actions (such as editing, publishing and deleting posts and comments) while being logged into the WordPress panel via the web interface. If you plan on removing the XML-RPC service on WordPress, then the ability to use any application that makes use of this API will be null. Disabling XML-RPC comes with a significant cost, given the fact that it plays an important role within WordPress nowadays. The possibility to disable XML-RPC has been limited, considering what a major API it is in WordPress, so by disabling it users could easily get confused and run into problems relating to applications that no longer work or have been broken given the absence of API access. JetPack is one of the most popular plugins for WordPress, which provides it with several essential functions, and this is primarily based on XML-RPC and will affect its proper functioning if another third party is used should you want to disable XML-RPC. While talking about these plugins, it is important to say that there are several of them that are available in the official WordPress repository, but as was previously stated, the functionality of applications that are highly dependent on it will be severely affected.

Some voices within the community consider that the backend of WordPress is well enough built, provided it can be accessed from any mobile device. This is why the majority of WordPress sites do not have the necessity for trackbacks, pingbacks, and the XML-RPC system implemented, which is why it deserves to be removed from WordPress. While we are impartial in regard to this view, it deserves attention as it brings up a logical point of view that states that it should be shifted towards a third-party that would no longer be set as default, in order to provide an improvement in security, the level of scalability and the stability of all WordPress sites and the platform itself.

The XML-RPC are requests that will be sent to the `xmlrpc.php` file which are present within the main WP installation directory . This simply does a bootstrap of loading which then moves on to creating an object of the class that is located within `wp-includes/class-wp-xmlrpc-server.php`, in this instance being responsible for handling all XML-RPC requests coming from the XML-RPC clients.

As a conclusion on XML-RPC support on WordPress, we can say that it will successfully enable automation of tasks on your WordPress or other client in performing remote tasks and features of XML-RPC that help WordPress to be an ongoing open and extensible platform.

REST API token-based authentication

Moving forward with developing REST APIs that require authentication, we will state that because the authentication itself will occur by some external service over HTPP dispense tokens will be used to avoid a repeated calling in the authentication service. In case you are debating using this method for basic HTTP Auth requests it is important to say that the advantage of a basic Auth solution is that you don't have to make a full-round request to the server and back before the requests for content can begin. These tokens can potentially be a lot more flexible and it will seem more appropriate to use the OAuth authentication in some contexts. Going further with authentication, it is important to say that base auto has the better advantage that it is a good solution at a protocol level, which means that BaseAuth user agents will recognize a password as one, preventing them from caching it.

The server load of Auth is going to dispense a token to the user instead of caching the authentication on your server, which you would be doing in this instance, with the key difference being that you are turning the responsibility for the caching towards the user, which is suggested should be handled with transparency on your server.

Regarding transmission security, it is important to say that if you can use an SSL connection than that's everything that is required for a secure connection, and to prevent multiple executions by accident you could filter out multiple URLs or ask users to include a random component within the URL.

Making sure your apps and sites are backward-compatible

The presumption has it that a REST API should always be backward compatible with a service that is being exposed to such interfaces, be those external or internal clients. In this part of our tutorial we will go through the meaning of backward compatibility and what exactly it means.

Backward compatibility implies the connection within two clients that have no conflicts of compatibility between APIs. During the report of a service to another, if the clients are not corresponding with their updates or versions of the API, then issues might arise.

It is perceived that client implementation will take some time to catch up with service implementation, thus not breaking the existing version of the API, even though it has been the subject of an upgrade. The purpose of backward compatibility implies that older clients should still work fine with a new version of the same API. While the old client will miss out the new features of the upgraded API, it will still be compatible with the features that correspond to it.

To ensure that a REST API will not break the backward compatibility, there are several steps we can take that could help us prevent this. The following are a few tips you might want to consider to assure the backward compatibility we have discussed:

- Additional HTTP response codes that will later be returned by the API
- The root of the URL or any existing query string parameters shall never be changed
- Other query string parameters will help towards good compatibility
- Mandatory or optional elements that are passed to the API will not be deleted
- Additional information that is added to the REST API must be optional

Backward compatibility in practice

Backward compatibility will have two primary functions that are going to be the backbone of the whole purpose of assuring backward compatibility:

- New functionality
- Preventing script breaking

We will see the preceding two functions briefly by the following:

New functionality

Backward functionality will permit the partial use of the new feature by moving the new API values, and if those are set as global within your scripts then it is very likely it will impact multiple sets of REST APIs. The impact on your existing scripts will be avoided if the new functionality will not be used, and for this, just stick to previous (existing) APIs. We should mention, if new APIs are not used backward compatibility might not be guaranteed from release to release and older functionality might be deprecated.

Preventing script breaking

To prevent our existing scripts from breaking and assure continuous functionality, we have to use the same API value for the specific REST API. Doing so will ensure that the same set of data will be sent and consecutively return in the response body during operations such as `POST` and `PUT`.

Releases of new REST API versions are a rare thing, which is why backward compatibility can often be assured by simply adding a new optional parameter or new method. If in your API you had a method and you were not satisfied with the way it functioned, there would be several ways to deal with it.

Adding a new parameter that would default to the initial one would make it backward compatible, and if it's necessary, a proper `if` condition might be applied. Refactoring your code is also a way by which old methods will call new ones internally but with modified parameters (and will re-format the results accordingly). Major releases of REST APIs will imply major changes in all of the methods used, and not just one. Most major REST APIs have never released a second versions of their API, this meaning that they still use version 1, and if you're sure about releasing the second version of your API, then new entry points have got to be created for all of your methods. This is what will cause you the biggest headache and stress regarding the technical approach you decide to take on this. Centralized APIs will usually increase only to indicate new features, and developers will often increase their version number to denote a major backward incompatibility.

RESTful services will not make use of versioning to provide change, given that this will reduce the ability to introduce new behaviors to clients. Maintaining compatibility with older clients is definitely a concern, and the way to deal with this is to make as few things as possible regarding your requirements in media type design and just add things that are optional later.

The future of REST API

In its current state, the REST API is used for a variety of purposes and is primarily meant to solve technical gimmicks that developers encounter on a regular basis. REST is a preferred choice for use in web applications where requests can be directed to any instance of a component, and thus its stateless can be quickly redeployed if something goes in the wrong direction. A cloud application is another direction that the REST API uses, and this is especially helpful in binding to a service via an API, which is simply the method of controlling the decoding process of a URL. If an application recognizes a micro-service by the URL, a simple change of the IP address that has been paired with the URL will easily let the request go towards a new instance if the component within the original one fails. The algorithms will distribute the requests if the URL is made to point towards a load balancer, as no request can handle the instance that keeps track of the state.

Another direction looking forward at REST API is the field of cloud computing and micro services, which will most likely make the design of the RESTful API a rule in future, which will favor developers who make use of the REST API.

Overall, REST is considered to be a secure method. However, there are voices that have manifested their concerns about how the components of an application are addressed via an open, VPN connection. The solution to this is the proper use of identity tokens, which can be a part of the RESTful API data package or simply a secure HTTPS connection, which should be more than enough. The scalability and integration with micro-services and REST are pretty broad, especially in virtualized applications. The support that REST has started to gain will provide you with the proof that the traction it has gained is more than enough to secure it a spot in further use by developers.

At this time, REST API is still facing quite a few issues that must be addressed and fixed. The team that is currently supporting REST says that they will fix the way comments, posts, users and terms are managed, implying that constant improvements and fixes will come. It is also stipulated that the REST API might become a way to store personal data, acting as a sole storage place.

The future of WordPress will be defined by the REST API, which will provide the possibility for WordPress to have even better integration with the rest of the Internet. The REST API is also set to become a core part of WordPress, but we shall get into this a little bit later.

The integration of the JSON REST API into WordPress will definitely represent one of the final steps in moving from a simple yet efficient blogging system to one fully-packed platform for applications that will be achieved by creating a homogenous interface that serves as a bridge between WordPress and any other software piece or application development that is currently available.

What will happen with REST in the future?

The future looks strong for REST API, as it continues to evolve and develop further. Let us see what the future holds for it.

PHP and WordPress

PHP has been and still is a veteran of the war relating to providing technical functionality for websites, and while this is still very much a fact, other programming languages that have proven their usability are now concurring with it. While PHP is a conservative, effective and well-known solution for many endeavors, it will admit the positive parts of other languages that will take its place, or at least be placed amongst it. REST API provides languages like Python and Ruby on Rails with instant access to the native functionality of WordPress, and with the frameworks available for those languages it is hard to imagine PHP maintaining its dominance for much longer. These frameworks of Ruby we are talking about allow amazing integration with other frameworks and will bring up some points for consideration.

Mobile integration

With the mobile era being the only actual thing nowadays, it is really important to assess how mobile integration and functionality play a huge role in the life of every application, system or website. WordPress, being the most used CMS on the Internet, will provide native applications that provide mobile integration with it, yet as it is common to be, third party integration is common as well. It is believed that by using the REST API, developers will manage to open a real backend for native mobile applications that will introduce new ways for future integration.

The backend

It is believed that the WordPress backend will be re-written, and with the integration of REST API in the core, the possibilities will be thought of in a different way, making it possible for developers to define their own unique way of using the administration panel, which is currently powered by the independent WordPress API.

REST API plugin versions

One thing to admit is that the 1.2 version of the REST API plugin is set to be the latest planned update that it will face, the focus being on the next, big version 2.0.

The team behind REST API is firmly committed to keeping the plugin as functional as possible, meaning that it will be supported in terms of backward compatibility. Its upcoming 2.0 version will emerge into the core of WordPress, and because of this the backward compatibility will be somewhat more limited than it is right now, yet a layer pattern of compatibility will be still maintained. Anything built using the plugin version will continue to work once the REST API is set in its core. The developers supporting it state that they will not be recreating the next version from scratch, and will try to keep things as they are for as long as possible, meaning that an eventual port from the current version to the new one would be a relatively simple process.

In its second version, the routes are supposed to be prefixed, and the core will use a `wp` prefix-custom routes using their prefix. The current use of the `wp-JSON` prefix will most likely be discarded, and older `wp-on` routes that are used by the client will be rerouted once they're placed in the core.

Another thing to look at is the fact that a potential universal API might be a reality. Furthermore, consistent behavior across different platforms needs to be ensured, so as to avoid usage issues and compatibility problems. One more goal for developers is to assure consistency across every platform and website for WordPress mobile applications.

Goals for REST API

One last goal that is set for the future of REST API is a solid foundation that has got to be fixed as soon as possible. The contributors behind REST API are set with the task of adding a RESTful API to millions of websites worldwide, while the structure and architectural build of these websites remain uncommon and unknown in their specifics, making it a daunting task. Besides creating a so-called ideal API that will work perfectly with an outrageous number of websites, another task is to implement and add a set of tools that will work as standard for anyone who's interested in making their own, functional yet generic API. It is expected that WordPress will work as a tool that will provide a point for starting a fully functional API that will be immediately ready to use, and whose customization will be a breeze.

The current state of progress with the JSON REST API will provide you with the ability to work around existing technical necessities, and to continue improving your skills as we wait for it to be implemented in the core of WordPress, representing the biggest update so far.

Limitations of REST API

REST, as a system in itself, is very predictable regarding endpoints and the content of the requests, being just an HTTP request. It is supposed that end-users can easily guess how to fulfill their aim as long as the URL structure of the site is familiar to them, which can be interpreted as a breach within the security system. This is considered one of the first drawbacks/limitations of RESTful APIs, but we will get to this in a minute.

Regarding performance, it is considered that SOAP is more advanced in this regard, making good use of event-based parsing, which adds to the scalability of SOAP stacks that use normal HTTP processing along the XML parsing, while REST uses the HTTP processing method alone.

Within the industry, there is a prolonged debate that denounces the security of REST related to other methods like SOAP, which is why some developers or clients choose to avoid REST. More technically-savvy developers or users would prefer REST, for the sole reason that its simpler approach is more appealing to them, yet as was stated, this is not the case for everyone. Overall, it is important to understand that absolute security cannot be reached, and it's your duty to make your application as secure as possible and avoid relying solely on the security measures of any of the APIs.

Given the architectural approach that is present within a RESTful system, we consider most of its properties to be useful only when used appropriately and for the developer, yet every positive point about REST has a drawback and limitation, which we will go over now.

In the client-server relationship, it is understood that the business logic is decoupled from any presentation, which means that changing any of those will not have an impact over any other, yet this adds some latency. The fact that REST by its form is stateless and the messages exchanged between client and server have all the necessary context means routing of messages is easy, but this again has a downside, which is more latency added and the messages that are being sent by the client have redundant information. If you are more technically savvy, REST provides you with the possibility to change many things server-side without having to do any rewriting of the code within the client, yet the drawback of this is the fact that if you commit mistakes during the implementation of the process, then you might get stuck and technical issues might arise. Overall, given the structure of the system, which is a layered one, you can change a lot of things and be provided with a lot of flexibility, yet, once again, this will add more latency on the server, so this is what you have to consider when making a decision about whether you are in favor or against-prioritizing what is more important for you, in the end.

At the end of the day, one of the biggest drawbacks there is in using REST is browsers that only support GET and POST methods, yet most firewalls only allow the passage of POST and GET methods. In case your app requires the possibility to run in these browsers you're doomed again, given that you're limited by the support REST provides. Regarding technical application, we understand that GET is used to retrieve information, PUT to update an already existing entity, POST to create a new object and DELETE to delete an existing one.

Another key point is that REST will not prescribe any of the HTTP verbs, and you have to build REST applications using HTTP only if you're cautious enough. It is thought that one good use of REST would be for primarily simple services and anything of the kind, such as a transformation service where the need for a lot of scalability and catching is not that great, and is thus acceptable.

As a conclusion on the limitations for REST API we should mention that it is not a good idea to use it for any applications that would imply retrieval and usage for real-time data. Another issue is the fact that if you capture every object from a stream, then you're set to have issues and difficulties as it is a tough job for REST to work with any high-throughput types of streams.

Summary

This brings us to the end of this chapter, as well as the book.

We hope you have had a great time learning about REST API and its association with WordPress. By now, you must have mastered how to send requests, read and modify data as well as perform complex queries using REST API on your WordPress site.

However, this book is just the start of your journey towards REST API. As time goes by, over the course of the coming years, REST API in WordPress will progress further, and more and more themes or plugins will make good use of it. As such, preparing right now and getting a command of it will help you get a head start in this domain.

As we close this book, it is advisable to implement REST API in your WordPress projects wherever you need to, but as the last section of this chapter discussed, be sure to keep the limitations in mind! That said, RESTful services are here to stay, and have been around for years, so being familiar with them will work in your favor.

Happy coding!

Index

S

T

U

W

www.ingramcontent.com/pod-product-compliance
Lightning Source LLC
Chambersburg PA
CBHW060556060326
40690CB00017B/3725
* 9 7 8 1 7 8 6 4 6 9 2 4 3 *